DON'T KICK THE DONKEY RIDE IT!

Wynne Goss D.div

Published by *in*HOPE Publishing

ISBN: 978-0-9567277-0-1

Published by *in*HOPE Publishing

Cover and Interior Design: CCD, London

Contents

Dedication

This book is dedicated to my children and grandchildren who, through the death of Anne, my first wife, have had their lives shaken and forever changed, yet are maturing though the process. Together we are learning that the Christian life is not to be lived event to event, but is a lifetime *process* of being changed from glory to glory into the likeness of Christ, learning to love Him and each other with His unconditional love.

What Others Are Saying About This Book

It is with great pride that I write these few words to recommend my friend and fellow minister Wynne Goss to you. In the first half of my twenty-three years of ministry I heard his name and ministry spoken of many times, although we never met personally. But his reputation as a pioneer, leader, pastor and man of God preceded him. In 2000 I had the privilege of meeting him for the first time and from there we grew in friendship and have worked together for the sake of God's kingdom ever since. Wynne was and is everything I had heard about him and, in my estimation, even more. His "coalface labor" and longevity in ministry qualifies him well to speak on the topic of this book. Here you will find not simply spiritual principles and some encouragement to live by them, but rather a testimony lived out by a man who inspires us to believe and trust in a faithful God. The author has progressed through his life and ministry trying and testing the truths outlined in this book, his momentum relentless and his advancing continuous, empowered by knowing how to ride his donkeys and not kick them.

- Hassan Boyle
Pastor, Grace Fellowship Family Church, Dundalk, Ireland

I highly recommend Wynne Goss' book. This is the testimony of a God-centered life. Not many people would dare to tell the whole story of their experience of walking through one of life's worst valleys. Reading his story caused me to rethink certain seasons of my personal journey, but it also caused me to believe and experience how God has the ability to turn the dark hours of our lives into victory. Read this message and be encouraged that you will make it through your own valleys. Thank you, Dr Wynne.

- Paul Godawa
Senior Pastor, Water of Life Church, Poland

I first met Wynne Goss in 1989. He was recommended to me by a prominent minister in England to participate in a Pastors Conference I was conducting at my pastorate in Riverside, California. I had no idea at that moment that a divine connection had been established. I traveled to Wales a few years later to minister in the two churches that he and his wife, Anne, had founded. It was there that I began to see his "world" calling as I observed the strong anointing of God's Spirit upon him. Since that time he has traveled to many nations preaching, teaching and bringing healing to multiplied thousands.

As I read Wynne's book I became aware of the attitude of victory that permeates every chapter and personal experience. His wife's battle with cancer, resulting in her home-going to be with the Lord forever, has strengthened his resolve to let people know that no matter what, God is on their side; God will see them through every difficulty that life on Earth has to offer. The grace of God, the unmerited, unearned, undeserved favor of God is clearly evident, and it is this grace that has sustained Wynne and his family through every difficulty.

God, in His favor, sent him a new love in Gwenda, whose love is not intimidated by the memory of Wynne's wife of his youth. She is committed to be the wife of their future together as she travels by his side and provides strength and understanding to a great man of God.

- Ron Halvorson
Senior Pastor, Bethel Church & Christian College, Riverside, California, USA

Having known Wynne Goss for seventeen years we not only wholeheartedly endorse his anointed ministry, but are grateful for the fact that he has been and continues to be a true friend. Throughout our journey he has not only imparted incredible truth into our lives and the life of our church, but has greatly inspired us by living out that truth on a daily basis. Wynne's life experience gives him a greater foundation to share the message that forms the chapters of this book, through which many lives have been and will be dramatically impacted and changed. The concept of accepting all that we go through, both good and bad, to be "purpose in disguise" is something that we need reminding of constantly as we navigate our way through life. This book will help you, challenge you, encourage you and inspire you in life to do whatever it takes and take whatever it does!

- Mike & Lois Radcliffe
Senior Pastors, Destiny Church, Bristol, UK

Bible teacher, man of faith, prophetic voice, fellow traveler, lover of Jesus, son of the Father. In this book you will meet Wynne in all the above facets. The revelation that is in this book is not theoretical, for Wynne writes with insights that come as a result of seeking to understand the events of (his own) life through the lens of the eternal. As he has journeyed with God you will discover that he imparts what he carries. I believe those who read this book will be drawn through their circumstances to stand in a new place – a higher place where new understanding will cause a spirit of thankfulness to spring up; a deeper place of faith that is grounded in the reality of knowing God's presence in their journey. For some, this book will be a literal life-changer, for others it will release an acceleration toward God's destiny, and I am sure that all who read it will discover the embrace of an eternal God who is their Father.

- Martin Scott
Author of Gaining Ground and Impacting the City

In *Don't Kick Your Donkey, Ride It!* Wynne Goss has written a book for people in pain, a book for the sorrowful who are wandering through the dark night of the soul, a book for those who have been disappointed in life and desperately need to recover hope. And an immensely encouraging and helpful book it is! It is both intensely biblical and deeply personal. Rooted in Scripture, Wynne speaks of his own journey through the grief of deep loss into a place of profound blessing and comfort. Wynne has been able to make this redemptive journey because Jesus made the same journey and invites us to follow Him. It's a journey where the agony of Good Friday is inevitable, but also where the joy of Easter Sunday comes as God's gracious surprise. For this reason I heartily endorse and urge you to read this remarkable book, and allow Wynne's journey with Jesus to mark the trail for your own journey to the place where you "let go of everything you have ever known to lay hold of everything you have dreamed of."

- Brian Zahnd
Senior Pastor, Word of Life Church, St. Joseph, Missouri, USA

Life seems to be made up of an unending series of valleys and mountain tops. We seem to constantly be climbing or sliding, depending on our direction. There is a lot of time spent in very deep water. In the animated film *Finding Nemo* the little blue fish, Dory, says, "The secret to life is to just keep swimming." She is so right.

Faith at all times is the key to success. Hope, rather than optimism, is what sees us through. The optimist believes things will get better "some day". The hopeful man sees Jesus in every situation "right now". When our hope is in the name of the Lord who made Heaven and Earth, we can always keep swimming.

I have been Wynne's friend for a long time. We have been through a lot together. We have laughed on the shinning mountain tops and guarded each other's backs in the midnight of the valleys. I've been there to see him live this book and it has been a privilege.

I'm sure this book will be a very useable tool for people who want move onward with the Lord. Thanks, Wynne, for taking the time to live this all over again on paper.

- Bishop Mike Warnke
Celebrations of Hope Ministry, Florida, USA

Acknowledgements

Thanks to my family and friends who went through the storms with me and to all those who from my beginnings taught and showed me His grace, free from condemnation or judgment.

To our faithful friends who, during the greatest season of transition in our lives, supported us financially, provided a home for us and a haven for me to complete the writing of this book.

Also my great thanks to Tim Pettingale for his patient, masterful work in editing this manuscript. You can have a great message to communicate, but it takes real skill to make it understandable and enjoyable. Thanks again, Tim.

To Pastor Ron and Annie Halvorson for constant support and guidance throughout the years and for continuous encouragement to stretch and reach for the fulfillment of our dreams.

To Dr Mark Chironna, whose preaching and insightfulness has been the inspiration behind this message.

To Pastor Rick Godwin, Dr Kelly Varner and Rev Kevin Connor – great authors and preachers whom God has used to impart so much of their gifting, knowledge and wisdom to me. God has used them to enable me to become the preacher and leader that I am today.

To the staff and students of *in*HOPE Academy who loved us dearly and served us tirelessly through one of the most challenging, yet impacting seasons of our lives. Their response to our message when dealing with their own "donkeys" was not only an inspiration, but a confirmation that the word burning in our spirit was timely and a powerful tool that would thwart the devil's greatest plans of destruction, and at the same time release within the hearts of every believer strength, confidence and trust to see the hand of God deeply at work during their darkest of moments. Many call it the dark night of the soul, but to me it means, "In one moment everything can turn around!"

To Gwenda, my beautiful wife, helper and devoted best friend, who forever sees the best in me, loves me unconditionally, brings me such joy continuously, labors tirelessly to fulfill the call of God upon our lives, and gives lavishly of herself to see the call of God in other people's lives come to fruition. A quiet, dedicated mother to hundreds of sons and daughters of the faith.

Foreword

We read in our Bibles that, in anger, Balaam kicked his donkey for not moving when a false prophet wanted him to move. The donkey had somehow seen into the realm of the Spirit and recognized that the Angel of the Lord was blocking the pathway that his master was taking. This donkey had insight into the dealings of God, while Balaam remained blind!

Similarly, so often we want to move forward in life in a way that makes sense to us, while God wants to take us in a completely different direction. But we don't want to be guilty of "kicking our donkeys", learning instead to cooperate with God's plans. In stark contrast to Balaam, Jesus came riding into Jerusalem on a young donkey – a sign of His absolute humility and surrender to the path the Father intended for Him, which included the cross.

Our ability to move from "faith to faith" and from "glory to glory" in our walk with God requires us to understand and embrace the dealings of the Holy Spirit in our lives that come because of the work of the cross. The prophet Habakkuk tells us that God "hides His power". It is because God hides His power that it is important to understand the subtle nuances and "behind the scenes" work of His Spirit in our lives. When we are going through a process it isn't always easy to understand what is actually taking place. It isn't until the process is over that we look back and gain insight into what the purpose of that process was. But once we grasp it we are prepared for a quicker, more adaptable response to God as we enter into the next phase of our lives.

God guides us through seasons in our lives and there are processes that He takes us through, even if at first we don't comprehend them or recognize the signs. While the sons of Israel only saw the acts of God, Moses learned His ways. Those ways are the processes of God. When we present ourselves to Him to be vessels fit for His use, we should expect some *processing* to take place.

If we are to find our way from one level of life experience to the next, we first have to *acknowledge* the process, before we even know what is taking place. Then we have to *embrace the process* by faith and hold fast to the power of the cross so that we can move through the process. Once we embrace the process we then need to *trust the process*. As we learn to trust the process that God is guiding us through we gain insight both about God and ourselves (as Job said, *"He knows the way I take"*) and as a result we can ultimately *enjoy the process*. All of this leads to the maturing of our lives, spiritually, emotionally and psychologically. Parts of us that need to die in order that we might be raised up to a new dimension of living are radically transformed. There is no way for this to happen, other than us cooperating with the process we agreed to when we gave our lives to Christ.

I consider Wynne Goss a dear friend who God allowed me to connect with during a season in my life, years ago, when I was first beginning to understand the processes of the Lord in my own life. When "bone comes together with bone", as in the vision of Ezekiel, there is a clear relationship between the two – the joint between the bones becomes an avenue of supply for the resources and provisions of God. Wynne is one of my "bones" in the kingdom. Over the years we have walked together through a number of stages of growth and development. I clearly remember the journey he and his first wife, Anne, walked through as she battled with cancer. Anne was a courageous soul that had unwavering faith in God and in His power. The fact that she battled for nine years was evidence to me that she was a seasoned warrior in the kingdom. When she passed, I watched as God brought Wynne and the family through their grief into coping with their loss. I also watched as the hand of the Lord began to work in fresh processes in Wynne to further establish his apostolic influence and measure of rule.

When it comes to the leading of God and the dealings of God, Wynne can walk you through those processes step by step with ageless wisdom and a perception born of God, who has given him rich prophetic insight. The book you now hold in your hands will take you, step by step, through the processes of God that take place in your life and lead you to a fresh place of peace and wellbeing. In a day when, globally, many are unsettled and uncertain, dealing with the rapid pace of unprecedented change, the truths in this book will help you both cope with the multitude of changes taking place in your life and empower you to profit from those changes. This is an era when God is sending a fresh wind of His Spirit through the weary places in our hearts and lives to bring us seasons of refreshing and restoration. What you read here will help you identify where you are in relation to the process you are going through. *Don't Kick Your Donkey, Ride It*, will be a key that unlocks the door to a new future for you in Him.

- Dr. Mark J. Chironna,
Mark Chironna Ministries, Orlando, Florida

Introduction

If you are looking to find a work of literary genius in the pages of this book, stop now! I am under no illusions about my literary abilities and have not written this book to fulfill some hidden ambition. Rather, this work is presented to release a prophetic word and bring insight that I believe will help the body of Christ worldwide to grasp something of that which God is doing in the earth today. Committing this message to print has not only helped me to distill it with more clarity than preaching it from a platform, but it will also, I pray, find its way into the hands of many I would otherwise never cross paths with.

The message of this book had been "brewing" in my spirit for many years, but finally came together during a refining process in my life carried out by the Holy Spirit when Anne, my wife of twenty-nine years, went to Heaven in November 2001 after a nine and a half year fight with cancer. In this book you will find an attempt to communicate what I discovered for myself during this season: that the events which unfold in our lives are the Lord's "messengers" – vehicles sent to transport us from our present sphere of knowledge, experience, revelation and grace, into a deeper understanding. The circumstances of life, if received correctly, have the ability to take us to higher and deeper levels in Christ, where we are set free from the things that limit us and hold us back.

This is not meant to be an exhaustive or complete work – the subject matter is too complex. But as you read, I believe the Holy Spirit will begin to open your eyes to what is happening in and around your life, and will help you to respond to Him correctly, instead of fighting His work in your life due to a lack of understanding on your part.

Prepare yourself for a swift and exciting shift in your walk with

God as He begins to show you that the "donkeys" that visit your life have the ability to *carry you* to your God-given destiny, helping you to be transformed into His likeness day by day.

- Wynne Goss
September 2010

CHAPTER 1

YOUR MISSING PEACE

Have you ever lost something and not been able to find it again, not realizing until it was too late how important and valuable it was to you? This is the painful truth that describes how many people live. Many of us seem to live our lives taking everyone and everything for granted until they are gone. We frequently fail to grasp how precious people, things and events in our lives really are, and instead place greater value on things that have no eternal value at all.

Twice during 1999, whilst in prayer, the Lord spoke to me giving me two very clear statements that gripped my spirit. Such was the intensity of these words that I knew there must be more to them than I initially saw. First, God said to me, *Don't kick your donkey, ride it!* Then, later that year, He told me, *Let go of everything you have ever known, to lay hold of everything you have ever dreamed of.* They were unusual words that were to become the two most significant words God had spoken into my life. Though I had no inkling of it at that time, these words would keep me steadfast through the most amazing series of storms and transitions ever to impact my life – and they still do.

I must be honest and say that, at the time, I thought I had just been given two great titles for a series of teaching messages I would preach in the church I pastored – and indeed, I did use them as the titles for a series of sermons. But after preaching them the messages remained strong in my heart. My next thought was that perhaps they could be the theme of a book. I began to put some thoughts down on paper, but soon reached the conclusion that a book was a project for "some time" in the future. Then, I recalled that I had been praying about the title and theme of our annual conference which would take place later that year and became excited because I believed God had put the answer to my prayers right in front of me.

Our annual conference came and went and all of our guest speakers ministered wonderfully on these themes. Yet, still my heart knew there was something more significant to be understood about what God had spoken. I resolved to seek Him and pray about this and I would not be satisfied until the Lord showed me clearly what it was all about. With my heart wide open for anything He might say, I sat at His feet until He gently whispered, "It's not a book title or a preaching series or a conference title. I am trying to let you know that this is about the journey of life ahead of you." With the passage of time I now understand a little of what God was telling me, but at that moment I understood little. I read excitement into those words, not the cost, confusion and challenges they would bring into my life and the lives of those closest to me.

Three donkeys

As a young boy I loved my father, but over time something in our relationship went sour and for a long time we didn't get along well. Things especially deteriorated once I became a born again Christian. Dad constantly argued and displayed verbal anger towards me and I constantly battled with resentment towards him in my heart. But, eventually the Lord did a miracle in both of our lives (more on this later) and in 1987 God healed our hearts towards each other and, from that moment on, my father and I had a wonderful relationship and friendship. He was my father, but he had now also become my best friend. In 1999 he died and went to be with the Lord. I grieved terribly. A part of me still wanted to make up for those lost years when the love and friendship had been non-existent.

Daily I visited my mother's home to make sure she was okay, but every time I entered the house I would see my father everywhere: in pictures, in the decoration, or in the way he had left the garden. Every visit seemed to have the ability to reduce me to tears. I missed him so.

The following summer my mother returned from a vacation explaining that she had spent the whole two weeks missing my father so much that she no longer wanted to live without him. She told me she wanted to be with him in Heaven. Just a few short days later she joined him there and my heart and life was struck by another major blow. In just one year the two people who had brought me into life, nurtured me, loved me and gladly sacrificed for me to have the best they could give me, were both gone.

My mum and I had the deepest and most loving of relationships and when I became born again she had the complete opposite reaction to my father's. She burst into tears of joy because it was the answer to a lifelong prayer that each of her children would become Christians and preach the Gospel of Jesus, just as her father had done many years before. In the midst of those tears she put her hand to her mouth and started apologizing to the Lord, because just weeks earlier she had become frustrated with Him and declared she was no longer going to pray for her children because He wasn't answering the prayers she had been praying for over thirty years. Now in front of her was His reply.

I consoled myself during this season of grief, telling myself I would be fine as I still had my wife, Anne, my two children, Matthew and Esther, my family, church and friends all around me. Life goes on! At this time, Anne had been battling breast cancer for something like eight years. We were Christians who believe in miracles and answers to prayer and had seen many such miracles over a twenty-five year period of ministry. Anne's miracle, we concluded, would surely come in due season. I was unaware that the "donkey" the Lord had spoken to me about in 1999 was about to visit my life a third time.

On November 21, 2001 my family and I stood around Anne's coffin saying our farewells, surrounded by hundreds of mourners. My children and I were holding onto each other, each of us stunned at this outcome, even though we had contemplated in our minds the unthinkable outcome of her actually dying. To the end we hoped beyond hope for her miraculous recovery, but she was gone. I was surrounded by a sea of faces, some blank, some hurt and let down, some filled with shock and disbelief. The unthinkable had happened. We did not get our expected miracle. Most had not planned for this outcome. Our church, and a multitude of churches and people around the globe, had been steadfastly praying for Anne's miracle, yet here we all were, facing not just her coffin but our deepest fears and unanswered questions. Everyone was silenced by the loss of a huge personality and influence on our lives with no answer as to why or for what purpose this had happened. Everyone believed the best outcome would have been for her to receive her miracle and be a testimony to God's healing power and grace. Oh, how we all had hers and our own lives planned out, so that when her death shattered them no one knew how to handle it.

I remember very little of that day. I floated numbly through the whole event trying to acknowledge the comfort of all the mourners, trying to stay tuned into conversations with friends who had traveled great distances to attend. My body was in the day, but my heart had withdrawn to try to find a place of safety and freedom from the pain I felt. I was reacting no differently than the prophet Elijah who ran from Jezebel to hide in the back of a cave (1 Kings 19:7-16). I was aware, more than at any time in my life, that having deep relationships brings with it the deepest of pain.

I was experiencing so much pain that I wanted to withdraw from people in some deluded way, thinking "no people = no pain." Of course, my heart was being completely irrational. When we withdraw to our comfort zone or perceived place of security, the pain is still there because it is within us.

Declining a visitation of Christ the Healer

Over the next few months I watched and noticed the different ways we all came to terms with Anne's death. Her death shook us to the core and affected us deeply. All of us were being forced to make the necessary adjustments to life without her, everyone finding it difficult, some impossible. Some were trying to live as if the tragedy had never happened, unwilling to talk about her or face dealing with the reality of a future without her. Anne's presence with us had provided us all with a certain peace. Now that she was gone it became evident that it was not just Anne who was missing, but our *peace.* Our lives, independently and collectively, were in turmoil. But we soon had to face the real truth. It was not Anne that we had taken for granted – although we probably did in many different ways – it was the peace we had known before her death, and suddenly it was gone.

Yet, God was looking to restore His peace in our hearts and help us to trust Him completely with our lives, in every season and situation. Never once during this time of pain was my faith tested, but my security was. The Holy Spirit's work was now to help me transfer my security from all I had known onto leaning on Him more than I'd ever done before. It was here, at this moment, in the midst of it all, that I understood Mark 11 so much more clearly than ever before.

In Mark Chapter 11 Jesus is about to face His greatest transition in life. He is about to be crucified and die. Here He takes time to reveal to His disciples that at the point of every great transition in life God provides a vehicle to carry you through your greatest and most painful experiences. He wanted them to understand that God always provides the victory for us and will perform the most incredible miracles – but only after the event has taught us every lesson it has to teach us. Jesus knew a donkey awaited His arrival at Bethany and Bethphage. It helped carry Him to the most painful event of His earthly life. But three days later, this same event turned the world upside down, opened the door of salvation that had been closed for millennia, and was the catalyst to an open heaven followed by 2,000 years of miracles as men and women began to call upon Jesus' name and serve His purposes.

Our "donkey" had certainly visited us, heralding a time of great transition and pain. But I realized that God had given us a choice. We could either kick this donkey, vainly refusing to accept its presence in our lives, or we could get on it and ride it, allowing it to carry us forward. We could let it break us or propel us forward, traumatize or teach us – the choice was ours.

My family, friends and myself were being forced to take a journey down a road called *transition*. Along the journey I watched the different reactions and mechanisms people used against circumstances beyond their control, i.e. the grief process. I discovered that the grief process exposed unresolved issues that people were afraid to face. Rather than deal with their pain and lack of peace, they used control mechanisms to protect themselves from facing them or the issue causing them. Their "blindness" caused them to run in fear from the experience that had come into their lives, not realizing it could afford them the opportunity to reconcile long held issues of the heart that kept them bound to the past and hindered their growth and maturity. Without realizing it, they had declined a visitation of Jesus Christ the Healer, whose sole desire was to restore to them their "missing peace".

Jesus' own disciples were similarly confused about the issues surrounding sickness and death. In John 9:1-7 Jesus heals a blind man and His disciples question Him, asking what caused the blindness. The framing of their question is revealing: *was it his own, his father's or his mother's sin that caused the blindness*, they wanted to know. It seems as though they needed to pin the blame on "someone" for something they didn't understand. They believed it had to be someone's fault. So it was when Anne died. Some were shaken so badly that they ended up quietly drifting from the church, finding it easier to avoid the pain and questions by staying away. But then they had to endure the comments of other Christians declaring them to be "backsliders" – people who should have reached out with understanding and loving assurance to draw them back into God's family. Others found a reason to blame *someone or something* for her death. Her sudden departure, aged just 50, didn't match their theology. They had no idea what to do with a situation that didn't fit into their biblical understanding. We all had to find a way through the dilemma of knowing a God who refused to sit nicely and neatly into our boxes of understanding, experience and theological perception. But man has always had this dilemma to overcome.

Transition through brutal, but honest words

One day in the first months of 2002, I sat in my dining room worshipping my Heavenly Father. I knew my help lay in remaining daily in God's presence, but once again I ended up sobbing uncontrollably. I never doubted God's love once during it all. I knew beyond doubt that He was faithful, but the loss of Anne hurt me so badly that I didn't know what to do with the pain. I was not angry with God, just truly grieving my loss.

I have known maybe three occasions in my life when Jesus has literally "appeared" in a vision to speak to me. There, in the dining room that morning, I experienced one of these visitations. He walked into the room, bent down by the side of me and laid His hand upon my shoulder as I cried out profusely to Him for help in coping with my grieving heart. But then He spoke the words I least expected Him to say:

"Why are you crying this time?"

I had been bent over, sobbing when He walked into the room, but after hearing this statement I found myself standing up, face to face with Him, ready to show Him my displeasure at what I perceived to be such insensitivity. It was the "this time" part that really annoyed me.

"This time?" I responded. I couldn't believe Jesus would need to ask me that. I was crying for the same reason I had cried every other day since Anne had died. "This time?" I replied sharply, "I am missing my wife, my lover, my best friend, my counselor, the mother of my children, the one I expected to grow old with!". Then came the bittersweet blow to my soul. "Well, she's not missing you," was His firm, yet loving response. I was so incensed by His words that I started to rant and rave at Him. Out came a flood of words and emotion as I sought to remind the God who knows all things of the sacrifices me and my family had made for Him in twenty-five years of ministry. He remained silent, letting me vent my frustration on Him until I stumbled and stalled, running out of steam.

Now, with yet more gentle but firm truthfulness, the Lord dismantled all of my defenses, reasoning and viewpoints. By the time He had finished the grief was gone and in its place came a torrent of praise to remain with me from that day onward. With the honest truth of a faithful friend He continued: "Anne is not dead, but alive – more alive than she has ever been on Earth. She is in Heaven, not Hell. She is no longer sick, she is healthier than at any time in her life. She is enjoying the answers to all her prayers and faith and she is not in your past, but in your future.

Now, what is the problem?" Before I could get a word out, He continued: "Why have you preached for twenty-five years how wonderful Heaven really is – that when you die you enter a place of perfection where there is no fear, guilt, rejection, hatred, envy, sin, sickness or poverty; that everyone who lives there does so in an atmosphere of total love, acceptance, peace, joy and wholeness? Yet, when someone goes there you are not happy about it!"

I was experiencing brutal, honest friendship from the One who cared enough to tell me it as it really is. Others were just empathizing with me, reminding me I was in deep grief and, of course, that was true. But He knew the difference between the natural grief I was meant to experience and my complete loss of perspective. I needed Him to remind me of the true, eternal viewpoint that would snap me out of the self-centered spiral that was keeping me trapped by my loss. I wasn't thinking about Anne's gain, I was too consumed by my "what about me" issues. Jesus' truth broke me open and set me free to move forward. Yes, I still grieved. Even while writing these few pages I have remembered those days with tears flowing as I let you into understanding a little of the most painful season of life I have ever known. But our greatest pain can become our greatest gain and from that moment on I stepped into a new level of trusting Jesus with every aspect of my life and began walking in a new experience of freedom from doubt because His peace had been restored to my heart. I had nothing to be afraid of. Jesus was more in control than I imagined. I had always believed with my theological understanding that He is always in control, but now I knew it with every fiber of my being. It was no longer just theology – now it was my experience. I was learning to walk in the joyous freedom of not being in control of *anything*, knowing that He was in control of every second of every day of my life and I need be afraid of nothing and no one.

In one moment Jesus had delivered me from trying to stay in control of everything into the wonderful freedom of knowing that nothing outside of me could harm me inside. He had transported me to a place of security and significance, and restored an inner peace in my life that I never even knew was missing.

Please come with me now on a journey where we will examine many different aspects of our walk with God and all that He revealed to me through this great transition in my life.

CHAPTER 2

FREEDOM –
ADAM'S ORIGINAL EXPERIENCE

*"And the LORD GOD commanded the man, saying, 'Of every tree
of the garden you may **freely** eat but of the tree of the knowledge
of good and evil you shall not eat, for in the day that you eat of
it you shall surely die.'"*
(Genesis 2:16)

Anyone who saw *Braveheart*, the blockbuster film of several
years ago, will recall the excruciating scene at the very end.
William Wallace had bravely led the Scots to rise up against their
adversaries, inspired by the belief of a better life, and the film
closes with the heartrending scene that reduced me (and no doubt
millions of others) to tears as Wallace cries out "Freedom!" while
the English torture him to death. His anguished cry expressed his
heart's desire for his people and nation to be returned to a state of
liberty. The Hollywood producers, I'm sure, did not realize that
this powerful sequence would not only resonate with the Scots'
history and heritage, but would strike a chord in the heart of every
human who yearns for the freedom mankind once enjoyed.

In the Garden of Eden, Adam had only ever known true and
complete freedom. He was "whole"; nothing was missing in his
life. He knew true liberty in every way. This was man's original
state. As long as Adam and Eve continued to shelter under the
authority and wisdom of God they remained in the blissful state
of freedom God had granted them.

When Adam sinned at the Tree of the Knowledge of Good and

Evil, he did not realize he had nothing to gain but everything to lose. He thought he was about to acquire something he didn't have. But when he sinned he gained nothing. Instead, he lost his freedom. Worse still, he *knew* he had lost it. The Genesis narrative reveals that as soon as Adam heard the sound of the Lord walking in the garden, he grabbed a handful of leaves from a fig tree and tried to cover up the fact he was missing something. Sin had entered Adam's life and created a barrier, an awkwardness, issues between himself and God, his Creator and faithful friend. It was not the fig leaves that created this barrier – they were just symptomatic of Adam's new state. They were the external evidence that revealed an inner change of heart.

Lost freedom exposes hidden slavery

Only when we lose our freedom in its fullest meaning and expression do we discover what we've lost and how much slavery there is outside of God's freedom. The immediate result of Adam's loss was that he went into hiding. He had never felt the impulse to hide from God before, so why now? The shame he felt caused him to hide behind a makeshift "mask" fashioned from things (the leaves) that he thought were "acceptable" to God, since He knew that God had called them "good".

"Then God saw everything that He had made, and indeed it was very good." (Genesis 1:31)

Adam believed he was no longer acceptable to God. Sin had instantly warped his understanding and perception, both of the Lord and himself. He believed he was no longer perfect and, if he was not perfect in every way, therefore unacceptable to God. He presumed the Lord would reject Him and be angry with him, so he hid his imperfection from sight. But from *whose* sight? Surely, not the Lords for He sees and knows all things. Adam's real problem was not how the Lord viewed him, but how he viewed himself. As Proverbs 23:7 explains:

"As he (a man) thinks in his heart, so is he." (Proverbs 23:7)

Adam was no longer acceptable to himself. He had failed and guilt rooted itself deep into his perceptions and belief system. Adam presumed the Lord would think like he did. He should have trusted God to work out the problem, but instead he hid his sin. He should have brought this error into the light, exposing it to the Lord's grace and loving-kindness, but instead Adam presented to the Lord (and everyone else) an "image" that seemed more acceptable to him. Today we have a world full of people imitating Adam's cover up; people who are afraid to be themselves, concerned more with image than reality and honesty.

The fact that Adam had staged a "cover up" was not the heart of the issue. The real problem was that he had accepted a lie as the truth. He believed that God his Father would not lovingly accept him as he was, despite his sin, nakedness and failure. This is the most erroneous and despicable lie that Satan has ever used to destroy lives. It is NOT the truth. The reverse is true! The message of the Gospel of Jesus Christ is all about the Father restoring us to a place called faith – *faith* to believe He is good and that He Himself, through Jesus Christ, has already paid the price for *all* sin. Through Christ we are restored to a full knowledge of His complete, un-diminishing, unfailing love for us.

When Adam lost the freedom to be himself he became bound, enslaved to the image he had manufactured. Whenever we are subservient to an "image" we have created to hide the real us, then anything that has the power to remove that image becomes a threat to us. The symptoms of that threat are fear and anger: fear of being exposed and anger because we can't control our circumstances.

The fruit of fear

*"I heard Your **voice** in the garden, and I was **afraid** because I was naked; and I **hid myself**."* (Genesis 3:10)

There are two things we can learn about Adam's reaction and perhaps our own in similar situations.

1. I hid myself

First it was Adam who hid himself – no one did it for him, the responsibility was his. But by hiding himself he had to try to become someone else. The more we try to be someone we're really not, the longer we delay the process of living the life God intended us to live. *Only you can live your life!* Real success in life is realized when we live in the grace of God to accept completely who we are and stop thinking the real us is not good enough. The work of Christ and His Spirit in our life is not just meant to save us from sin – it is also intended to *release us* from sin's perverted lies which bind us like creeping ivy: covering us up, restricting us and preventing us from moving forward. It is the work of the Holy Spirit to uncover the real us from underneath everything we've covered ourselves up with – to release us from the image we've convinced ourselves is more acceptable to God and others than who we really are.

We see the results daily all around us: women and young girls are driven to look a certain way to please men and compete with the super model imagery that pervades the media. People in debt attempt to live to a standard they can't afford in order to aspire to and maintain a certain image. Even pastors of churches lie about the size of their congregations because a "big" church is perceived as a successful church and they want to project a successful image! But real success is discovering the freedom to simply be yourself, not someone else.

We have a world full of people who are all trying to be the opposite of who they are. Each example on its own seems insignificant, but when we consider the myriad examples life throws up at us, we can only conclude that it is evidence of the same inner problem Adam had. We have white people desperate to look darker skinned, tanning themselves to the point of endangering their health. We have dark skinned people bleaching themselves to look white. Those with curly hair wish it was straight and others with straight hair want theirs to be curly. Women with big breasts are looking to reduce them, while others are getting implants to make theirs bigger. Presently this fashion has even moved into the realms of buttocks and lips! We have tall people doing everything they can to seem smaller and small people doing the opposite. We have men having operations to become "women" and vice versa. And so the list continues – and for what? The "acceptable image" that everyone craves simply does not exist. It is an idealistic concept that exists only in the mind of the individual. But all this hiding and posturing can cease the moment we allow ourselves to fall in love with who we really are and accept ourselves as Christ accepts us. We will never have the power to change until we first accept who we really are.

2. I was afraid

Adam tells us why he covered himself up: *fear.* Fear? Of what? Hebrews 2:15 gives us an insight:

"Those who through fear of death were all their lifetime subject to bondage."

What had the Lord promised Adam if he ate from the Tree of the Knowledge of Good and Evil? Death! Adam knew before he sinned that every sin must be punished and there was a price to pay. Death was the cost. He was instantly afraid to die. But the real Adam had already died. It was a "fake" Adam who now took his place. The real Adam would never truly, fully live ever again.

But fear was not the first thing Adam experienced after he sinned. In order to be afraid we must first believe that we are guilty of doing (or being) something worthy of punishment. Fear has to do with punishment.

*"There is no fear in love; but perfect love casts out fear, because fear involves **torment**. But he who fears has not been made perfect in love." (1 John 4:18)*

The word "torment" used in this verse by John the apostle means "punishment" or "penal affliction". It shows us that fear flows out of the root of guilt, caused by the knowledge that we have failed or the belief that we are a failure and the outcome will be punishment.

The moment Adam sinned his simple trust and faith in the Lord was demolished. Peace left his heart and shame and condemnation flooded in, along with guilt, to convince him that the Lord would reject Him. Turmoil entered his spirit where previously only peace had reigned. He felt naked and ashamed. A wall of faith in his heart had been breached and a torrent of satanic lies had entered the sanctuary of peace he had always known. He had never known one thought of failure, anxiety, hatred or shame. But everything had changed!

John the apostle shows that fear is the absence of the knowledge of God's perfect love. What Adam lost, therefore, was the assurance of God's complete, perfect, unfathomable and faithful love towards him, even in his sin. He now believed the Lord would only love him if he was perfect in every way! Is this you? Have you ever felt like Adam? Have you tried to fit into everyone's little "box" of acceptability? If you haven't realized it already, there is no "box" of acceptance, only a coffin of despair.

You can *never* be everything everyone else wants you to be, not least because they can't make up their minds what that is – it changes with people's moods and circumstances. I can tell you what people need you to be, however: *the real YOU!*

The curse of self-righteousness

If you think you can do something to lose God's perfect love, then you will automatically believe you can do something to earn it back. This is called "self-righteousness". Adam's gathering of fig leaves and sewing them into some sort of garment to cover his nakedness was man's first attempt at religion. Religion is man trying to make himself acceptable in order to please God. In stark contrast to religion, Christianity is about God coming to man and making us perfectly acceptable to Him. He does it by asking us to *believe* in Him and His Word through faith in the blood of Jesus, God's perfect Lamb, which was shed at Calvary. Acceptance cannot be achieved by anything we can "do" at all. We cannot make ourselves perfect by any means, so God *makes* us perfect and acceptable to Him when we put our faith in the blood of Jesus and nothing else.

Adam's nakedness was an issue of the heart, not the absence of a covering. He had lost the peace that came through trusting God completely with his life. Four thousand years later Jesus stood up and said,

*"Come to Me, all you who labor and are heavy laden, and I will give you **rest.**"* (Matthew 11:28)

And Paul the apostle reminds us that, *"He Himself is our peace"* (Ephesians 2:14).

Jesus is God's peace restored to us. If we are born again the Bible says we are "in Christ". Therefore we are restored back to His peace, the peace Adam lost in the Garden of Eden. This peace can only come by knowing that we are completely and undeniably loved with a perfect love. The perfect love of God is just that! It is perfectly consistent towards us every day, no matter what we have done or how we feel. God's love is always the same towards us, even when we have failed.

"Jesus Christ yesterday, today, forever the same." (Hebrews 13:8)

We cannot "lose" the love of Father God. We can reject it or not receive it, but He will never stop loving us! If we choose to walk away or reject Him and end up in hell, that is our free choice, but it does not stop His constant love towards us – that is unconditional. There are no conditions to His loving us – He just does. God has chosen to love you and me whether we love Him in return or not. And the measure of His love for us is seen in the greatest demonstration of love ever seen: Calvary and a brutal cross. The reason God desires us to accept His great love for us is not for His benefit at all, but because He knows it will set us free and save us from enduring horrendous pain in life and in death.

If you have never accepted God's love for you in the way I am mentioning, then right now put down this book and take a moment or two to talk to Him. Ask Him to forgive you for never understanding or receiving His great love for you. Ask Him to save you and wipe away all of your sinfulness and fill your heart with His love. Offer Him the rest of your life to serve His purposes. He will give you a new life, wiping the slate clean of all your failures, and His Spirit will begin to help you know Him and guide you to live a great life with Him.

CHAPTER 3

TAXING TIMES CAN
PRODUCE MIRACLES

The manifestation of God's greatest miracle and intervention in the history of mankind came during an intensely stressful time in the lives of Joseph, Mary and the nation of Israel. Jesus was born in the midst of adversity, His early days on earth a prophetic glimpse into His last days. It was a time when Israel was in conflict with the Roman authorities. Caesar had commanded that every citizen must be counted in a census and a heavy tax levied upon each subject. This is why Joseph and Mary were returning to Joseph's home town of Bethlehem. Jesus was born into "taxing" times.

Thirty-three and a half years later, while enduring the cross and the complete rejection of man, He could look back to His beginnings and see the journey on which God, His Father, had led him. He understood the truth that our greatest apparent setbacks can be God's greatest set-ups for our greatest ever breakthroughs.

"... Jesus, the author and finisher of our faith, who for the joy that was set before Him endured the cross, despising the shame ... has sat down at the right hand of the throne of God."
(Hebrews 12:2)

The Bible tells us that as Jesus hung on the cross in complete agony, He did so looking forward to the great joy that was set before Him – a joy so expansive that it was enough to help Him endure His brutal crucifixion. How incredible that joy must have been in order to exert such a grip on His heart, mind, emotions and will, that He willingly embraced the suffering and humiliation of being stripped naked, stripped of His dignity, stripped of everyone and everything that was precious to Him – including a Heavenly Father who had turned His back on Him at that point – as well as the physical pain that would ultimately lead to His death.

Jesus knew that the greater the cost, the greater the ensuing miracle and victory. The cross was His greatest pain and battle. As He gave the greatest gift He could give – His very life blood – He let go of everything He knew to lay hold of everything He had ever dreamed of. God was granting Him His greatest desire: that all men everywhere would hear His gospel, receive His forgiveness for their sins and receive His very nature. As a result of His sacrifice, His followers could be filled with the same Spirit that would raise Him from the dead. They would be able to walk in the same power over sin and sickness, break free of every fear and doubt, and reign with Christ in God's presence eternally.

Jesus knew that His death and resurrection would open the way for the salvation of all mankind, even though it meant Him paying the greatest price He could pay. The rewards that lay ahead compelled Him to overcome everything that would try to prevent it coming to pass, until His victorious defeat of Satan's power was accomplished and His thirty-three year earthly journey was completed at Calvary.

We need to know that in the same way, our greatest miracles are frequently conceived during the most "taxing" situations and circumstances, and frequently come to fruition at the point of our greatest testing and pain.

Focus Daniel-san, Focus!

Some years ago, when I was pastoring a church in Wales, I was preparing a message to deliver on Sunday morning and trying to think of a good title for it. The topic was how to stand on the Rock during the storms of life. I wanted a catchy title that would help people remember it, but I just couldn't think of one. I prayed that the Lord would inspire me in due course and then left my study to join the family.

Matthew, my son, asked if I wanted to watch a movie with him, so I grabbed some food and headed for the couch to enjoy some time with him, not knowing what we were going to watch. It turned out to be the TV premiere of a new movie, *The Karate Kid.* This classic movie is familiar to many (and has recently been re-made for a new audience). It follows the story of a young man, Daniel, who moves to a new town with his single-parent Mum, but suffers bullying at the hands of local thugs. But he meets an old man who is an unconventional martial arts expert and during the course of the film, Mr Miyagi teaches Daniel how to defend himself, eventually entering him into a Karate competition, knowing full well he will face the boys who had bullied him for so long.

The last stages of the film show Daniel in the final contest with the ring leader of the bullies and Daniel is losing on points. He is about to give up because he feels he cannot overcome his opponent. Right at that point, Mr Miyagi runs to the side of his protégé and challenges him firmly with the words, "Focus Daniel-san, focus!" He had identified Daniel's greatest opponent: it was not the boy standing before him, but the negative thought patterns that encumbered his mind. Daniel was consumed with thoughts of failure. Mr Miyagi recognized that such thoughts were rooted in past failure and had no bearing whatsoever on the current battle in his life. With Miyagi's help Daniel managed to focus on his present challenge and quickly gained new confidence, defeating his opponent in a few, deftly executed moves to become the new champion.

At the end of the film I leapt to my feet. I had my title! I would call my sermon "Focus Daniel-san, Focus". The next day as I shared the opening comments of my sermon, I stood on one leg, imitating the Karate "crane form" that Daniel had adopted as Mr Miyagi uttered his immortal words. The church broke into laughter and applause as they realized what I was doing (most of them had also seen the film the night before) and my goal was achieved. For many years afterwards people recalled this message due to its title and visual demonstration! I told people what the Lord was asking them to do when facing their greatest challenges in life: to *focus* on His Word and the truth that He turns *everything* around for good in the lives of those who love Him. In other words, out of taxing times come miracles.

*"And we know that **all things** work together for good to those who love God, to those who are the called according to His purpose."* (Romans 8:28)

In your Bible the word "His" in this verse will be in italics. The translators have rendered it this way because in the original Greek letters the word *His* does not appear. They included it because they felt it made more sense grammatically and gave the reader a clearer understanding of what the writer was trying to say. If you remove this word, then the verse reads,

"…all things work together for good to those who love God, to those who are called according to purpose."

This small adjustment doesn't create a significant theological change, but for me it brings a slightly different emphasis, which is this: the moment we begin to walk and work to fulfill the purpose God has for our life, then everything that happens begins to turn around for our good. Even the negative stuff that happens to us becomes the thing that God uses to propel us forward or in some way help us towards the purpose for which we were created.

Jesus knew this principle. He knew His ultimate purpose was to be the Lamb of God who would be slain to pay for the price of man's sin. He knew that everything around Him, good or bad, would work for the ultimate achievement of this goal as long as He stayed focused on His purpose.

Transfixed or Transformed?

Read the following account of Jesus' transfiguration:

"Now after six days Jesus took Peter, James, and John his brother, led them up on a high mountain by themselves; and He was transfigured before them. His face shone like the sun, and His clothes became as white as the light. And behold, Moses and Elijah appeared to them, talking with Him. Then Peter answered and said to Jesus, 'Lord, it is good for us to be here; if You wish, let us make here three tabernacles: one for You, one for Moses, and one for Elijah.' While he was still speaking, behold, a bright cloud overshadowed them; and suddenly a voice came out of the cloud, saying, 'This is My beloved Son, in whom I am well pleased. Hear Him!' And when the disciples heard it, they fell on their faces and were greatly afraid. But Jesus came and touched them and said, 'Arise, and do not be afraid.' When they had lifted up their eyes, they saw no one but Jesus only. Now as they came down from the mountain, Jesus commanded them, saying, 'Tell the vision to no one until the Son of Man is risen from the dead.' And His disciples asked Him, saying, 'Why then do the scribes say that Elijah must come first?' Jesus answered and said to them, 'Indeed, Elijah is coming first and will restore all things. But I say to you that Elijah has come already, and they did not know him but did to him whatever they wished. Likewise the Son of Man is also about to suffer at their hands.'" (Matthew 17:1-13)

When the disciples saw Jesus' transformation they were transfixed. Their response, when all the action was over, was to set up a memorial so that everyone would know what had happened at this place. They thought it was the most incredible thing they had ever seen and could not believe things could get any better than this; they wanted to remain where they were and not lose this moment. How like the disciples we are! So many of us experience God in wonderful ways, but instead of realizing that our relationship with Him can just get better and better, we stay rooted at the place of our last great experience and set up camp there. This is how our personal growth in Christ is stunted. This is how living, breathing Church movements become institutions, entrenched in past experiences, afraid to move forward into the new things that God is doing now.

What incredible manifestations of God's glory and power have been prevented because a portion of the Church has stood still at the place of their revelation, built a fortress, and resisted everything else God wanted to do from then on, believing themselves to be the last bastion of real truth while everyone else was in error? Imagine what our world would be like today if Church streams had never divided over "revelation" and had kept on moving forward into all God had for them. Imagine what miracles are prevented because Christians insist on chaining themselves to past experiences instead of believing God has more for them than they could ever receive. We must not become "saved, satisfied and stuck"! We must continually move forward and leave our past experiences behind, no matter how good or bad they were.

Moses and Elijah had not just turned up to give the disciples a spiritual experience, but had come with divine purpose. From this point in His ministry onwards, Jesus focused Himself on heading for Jerusalem for the final time. Just like Mr Miyagi stood alongside young Daniel and spoke words that focused him, so Moses and Elijah did the same for Jesus. His mind was now focused on His ultimate purpose and His face set like flint, immoveable. Nothing would distract Him from finishing the course that had been set before Him and all things would turn for His good along the way, even though He knew He would face His greatest trials and affliction from this point onwards.

Remember, just like Jesus, God can accomplish the same miracle for us. Our greatest apparent setbacks can be God's greatest set-ups for our greatest ever breakthroughs.

CHAPTER 4

YOU CAN RUN,
BUT YOU JUST CAN'T HIDE

It was not by chance that Moses and Elijah were sent by God at this moment in Jesus' life. He was fully aware of the significance of the moment. Moses was the "Law-giver", the one who had written the Pentateuch, the first five books of the Bible. Elijah was a prophet, yet more than just a prophetic ministry. Elijah's life and spirit encapsulated and symbolized all of the prophets and all God had said to His people through them from the beginning until now. In other words, it was not just two great men of God who stood alongside Jesus at this point, it was the "Law and the Prophets" (Matthew 22:37-40; John 1:45). The Law and the Prophets was a name that, at that time, referred to the whole of what we now call the Old Testament. Neither of these men had experienced that which they knew Jesus was about to endure, though both knew what it was to go through a season where they bore their own "cross" – in their case a complete death-to-self in order that they accomplish the will of God.

It is imperative for us to understand right now that just to fulfill the will of God is not enough! We must also have God's motivation. To fulfill God's will in God's way with God's motive we must truly be emptied of every selfish motivation and egotistical need before we can accomplish that which He has set before us. Moses and Elijah had both been through this process and relinquished all motives of vengeance, dominance, control, prejudice, self-preservation and the need for man's approval. As a result God was able to use them to deliver His people. To understand this more, let's take a closer look at Moses' life.

The bigger the need, the greater the seed!

Moses was born in the midst of a time of great torment for the people of Israel. They were in need of God's deliverance. The Egyptians had enslaved them and burdened them with building Pharaoh's pyramids, palaces and promenades. But the more Egypt afflicted them, the more Israel increased in number until Pharaoh, fearing that Israelites may eventually outnumber Egyptians, decreed that all male children born must be *"cast into the river"* to die (Exodus 1:22). At this terrible time a girl called Jochebed, Moses' mother-to-be, realized she was pregnant by her husband. It would have been a joyous occasion at any other point in history, but she was filled with mixed emotions, wondering whether it was a girl or a boy. If the baby was a girl they would be relieved, but if it was a boy …. the consequences were too dreadful to consider. As the months advanced, so the couple's conversation increasingly turned to discussing their fears.

Doctors today tell us a child in the womb hears, senses and feels everything through their mother. The child does not understand the language spoken, but interprets the emotions those words convey. Expectant parents, therefore, are encouraged to speak daily to their unborn child as it provides comfort and the child learns, even before birth, how their parents feel about them. Moses' parents conversation, filled with fear and anxiety over what gender their baby is would be having an effect on him. Moses sensed their uncertainty. He sensed it would be a relief to them if he was a girl rather than a boy. How many messed up sons and daughters do we have in the world today because their parents wanted desperately to give birth to the opposite gender, thereby enslaving a child to forever trying to be all their parents wanted, even if it means throwing aside who God made them to be?

A few months later all the speculation was over and their fears became reality. The baby was a boy. Moses' mother was emotionally torn. She just wanted to hold and love her baby like any normal mother, yet she knew she faced the torment of releasing him to certain death. Joy and grief were mixed at that moment. Hearing the news that his wife had delivered a son, Moses' father, Amram, hung his head in despair. His eyes filling with tears he let out a deep cry from within, "Oh God, no, not a boy!" He knew the brokenness that he and his family were about to face. Again, his words must have reached the ears of newborn Moses, still in the arms of the midwife – words of despair that pierced his soul.

The Hebrew midwives did everything they could to hide male children from watching Egyptian eyes, so Moses was dressed to look like a girl. A veil was hung in the back of the house so his mother could feed him out of sight, in an attempt to protect him. To Moses this was confusing, reinforcing the idea that he was unacceptable as he was. Every time he cried in pain or because he was hungry his mother, in fear of his life, nursed him and probably did to her son what millions of mothers have done to their children – gently tapping his lips with her fingers, saying, "Shh!" and encouraging him to be quiet so as not to attract unwanted attention. Could this be why Moses was a stutterer in later life? Had he been impacted by the sense that his parents wanted to hide him away and silence his voice? Was this why he had no confidence in speaking out? (Genesis 4:10) It seems as though all that was being done to protect this child would have longer term negative consequences.

Through these days and months Moses' parents cried out to God for help, for wisdom and deliverance from their situation. Before this event in their lives they may have thought, along with others in Israel, "Where is God in all of this?" or "If God really loved us He would intervene and do something about Israel's situation." But now that general anxiety had become a personal need for a miracle and they were urgently prayerful. It is amazing how often we have to be brought to a place of personal need requiring a miracle before we truly turn our hearts to God and pray with diligence and urgency. It is often the painful situations of life that reignite a passion for Him that has become dormant as other things have become more "important", or ignites in us a passion we never had.

Placing your faith in His Word

As these dear parents pleaded with God for His miracle answer, one of them sensed deep within that this child was somehow the long awaited deliverer of Israel. Then together they experienced a growing sense that their baby boy would be saved from death to accomplish God's destiny for his life. A real peace and joy must have flooded their hearts. But they still did not know how this would be achieved. They continued to pray until one or both of them knew what must be done. God's solution? The baby must be placed into the River Nile. Oh, how unthinkable! They were asking God to save their son and His answer was to release him to almost certain death? But there are times when, in order for our prayers to be answered, we have to trust God like we have never trusted Him before. This couple needed the greatest miracle of their lives. God's way required them to take the greatest step of faith they had ever taken and pay the greatest price they would ever pay to get it.

I can only imagine what they felt when the terrifying moment came for the baby to be placed in a basket and cast onto a river filled with crocodiles and poisonous snakes. Their son would not have understood with his mind what they were doing as they kissed him goodbye, tears streaming down their faces, not knowing how to endure the pain. But he would have sensed with his heart that they were abandoning him, confirming his deepest fears that he was not acceptable.

I ask you, at this moment, to put yourself in their shoes and to feel a little of what they felt as they stepped out in faith, trusting God and complying with His will for their lives. Somehow God had brought them to a place where they trusted His ways above their own, His wisdom rather than theirs, despite the pain they would have to endure. Jochebed placed her son in the Nile and gently let him go, her heart breaking, those near her holding her back, preventing her from changing her mind and jumping in immediately to retrieve him. How painful to cast away something so precious that she loved so much. Since she could not chase him down the river, she did the only thing she could do: she ran home screaming, trying to escape the pain. But the truth is, we can run, but we just cannot hide from such pain. Ironically, we run from that which we are afraid to face, not realizing it has the potential to give us back what our hears are crying out for – and God knows it! On the other side of our greatest fears lie our greatest miracles. But we have to face that which we don't want to face in order to receive them.

Moses had a sister, Miriam. With her mother absent, this young girl was left to watch her baby brother's basket as the river took it quickly downstream. What would happen? How was this God's answer? But then, inexplicably, the basket began to move towards the river bank. It was moving closer and closer, in fact, to Pharaoh's palace. Miriam was afraid because she should not even have been in that area as a Hebrew salve, but she desperately wanted to see what would happen to her brother. The basket settled in amongst the reeds right near the place Pharaoh's daughter liked to bathe during the day. It came to rest precisely at the moment when Pharaoh's daughter and her entourage were arriving there. Moses and Pharaoh's daughter were being drawn together by God because of destiny. Often in our lives we cannot see that apparently negative situations are, in fact, pulling us towards our destiny.

At this moment I believe an angel stirred the basket and whispered to the baby to cry. Moses readily did and it gained the attention of the appropriate person, Pharaoh's daughter. The young girl heard the cries of the baby and someone was dispatched to find the child. Eventually he was discovered and brought to her. The basket was opened and there lay a child whose eyes were full of tears from the fear of abandonment, needing to be accepted by someone. Instinctively his hands reached out towards her and just as instinctively she reached out to hold and console him. But Moses was inconsolable. It would take more than a few hugs and kisses to settle and comfort him. Plus it would take a real mother to feed him and Pharaoh's daughter knew it.

So did Miriam! Before anyone could make a move, Miriam popped up from her hiding place and volunteered to fetch a Hebrew mother who still had milk in her breast so the baby could be comforted. With permission granted, she rushed as fast as her legs could carry her, one minute crying out of sheer joy and relief, the next minute screaming to her mother to come quickly before the opportunity passed. For a miracle to happen, you must be prepared to act immediately when the Lord provides an opportunity.

Miriam was grasping and pulling at her mother, trying to explain what had just taken place, but her mother couldn't understand – she was still overwhelmed by the grief of letting her baby go into the Nile. Miriam kept on persuading her that Moses was rescued and all would be well if she just trusted her and followed her down to the river to meet Pharaoh's daughter. "Pharaoh's daughter?" came the reply. "Pharaoh's daughter? She could kill me!" But Miriam persisted and eventually managed to lead her mother along the path to meet Pharaoh's daughter.

"Can you feed this baby?" enquired Pharaoh's daughter. "Yes I can," Jochebed softly and fearfully replied. So, incredibly, Moses was handed over to his own mother. The moment Moses lay in his mother's arms he knew her familiar smell and although he was sobbing profusely, his mouth opened to receive her breast. Mother and son were together again. As Moses lay in her arms, tears filled his mother's eyes, trickled down her cheeks, and her heart cried out a silent prayer of thanks to God for saving her son. All around her were aware of the way this baby had taken to this woman and no one was surprised when Pharaoh's daughter announced she would employ her to nurse this new "son" of hers.

Your seed pulls you towards destiny

Those in Pharaoh's service were dressed more gloriously than princes in other countries, so something had to be done about this woman's appearance. She could not enter the palace looking like a slave. Moses' mother went through a crash course on palace etiquette. She had to bathe in the oils of Egypt's finest perfumery and was given the very best food to make sure that this "royal son" received the very best of everything. In one moment Moses' mother had been transformed from being a slave living in a hut in poverty, having lost her son, to being a mother again, clothed in Egypt's finest silks and satins, eating the very best cuisine, and allowed to move freely in and out of Pharaoh's palace. Her greatest pain had become the door to her greatest gain! Her setback had become God's set-up, not just for Moses' benefit but also her whole family. She had received an answer to her prayers for the safety of her son and at the same time been transferred from a life of poverty to prosperity. And more was to follow!

The big cover-up begins

For the rest of his young adult life Moses was raised as an Egyptian, the grandson of Pharaoh. He dressed, looked, ate, walked and talked like an Egyptian. But during those early years when his mother nursed him, she sang the songs of Israel over him and whispered daily into his ears that he wasn't an Egyptian, but an Israelite, a child of God, a mighty man of God, Israel's deliverer. Now much older, he couldn't fully remember his mother's words, but they were planted deep within him and one day they would erupt to the surface.

As he grew to understand Egyptian ways Moses learned more about the daily life of the nation, especially the building work and other tasks the Israelite slaves were forced to carry out. Slowly but surely the words his mother placed in him as a child became louder and louder, convincing him that he was called to lead Israel out of captivity back to the land of Canaan that Abraham had said would be their land. But each time those thoughts began to grip his heart he would subdue them and push them back down, thinking them ridiculous. Each time they disturbed his conscience he was faced with the pain of the past.

Even though his mother and he had been re-united by God's miraculous intervention, embedded in his emotions were the doubts and fears of rejection that he felt as a child. Moses battled with his self-esteem, always believing Israel would never receive him as their leader and deliverer. Moses' real battle wasn't whether his family or Israel would accept him, however, it was whether *he would believe* he was acceptable. We can be rejected by everyone around us, but it doesn't mean we have to believe we are a reject. That is our choice and is not dictated by the actions of others. In life we can never control all that happens to us, but we can control how we respond. It doesn't matter what others say or think about us, it's what we think about ourselves that is really important.

Moses was dealing with a divided life: he had two identities, was immersed in two cultures and kingdoms, and constantly heard two conflicting inner voices. What would he do? Was he going to be a citizen of Egypt or Israel? Would he live in the past or take hold of his future? Would he be swayed by man's actions or God's word? The longer this inner conflict raged the closer he came to being forced to choose. Eventually, God had to engineer a situation to make him choose.

Weekly Moses walked among the Israeli slaves, their sounds and smells all oddly familiar to him. Each visit to their camp became longer and more frequent as his inner voice of destiny spoke louder and clearer. This went on until one day he was confronted by the sight of an Egyptian beating an Israeli slave. As the Egyptian's punishment was meted out with more and more violence, two voices within Moses vied for attention. The voice of his childhood and early Jewish beginnings cried out for him to intervene as the deliverer of God's people, while the voice of his Egyptian upbringing told him to be logical, reminding him of the rejection he had suffered at the hands of the Jews.

"You are a Jew!"

"No, you are an Egyptian!"

The argument went back and forth in a split second until he could contain the conflict no more. Instinctively he attacked and killed the Egyptian. The spared slave ran off to tell everyone what had happened. Moses, stunned by his actions, still shaking from the moment, hastily buried the dead man's body. But it was not just the Egyptian's body he laid to rest in the sand. Under the earth he buried both his guilt *and* his dreams. He would return to this desert to resurrect them some forty years on in his life.

The more you run the greater the problem becomes

In fear for his life Moses fled from both the Egyptians and the Israelites. Neither people group wanted him now. Both mistrusted him. His problem had got worse. He had struggled to overcome the fear of rejection by his Israeli family, but now his Egyptian family would reject him and want to kill him. He went deep into the wilderness wondering what to do next. As he journeyed further he drew near to a water hole and there confronted some shepherds who were intimidating and driving away seven sisters who were trying to water their father's flock. Soon Moses had brought the girls and their father's flock to the water and was helping them make sure the flock had their drink. Moses had no idea that this was another moment of destiny happening to him. So often we think a moment of destiny is going to announce itself with flashing lights and voices from Heaven declaring that this is God's destiny for us, but that is not how it usually happens. Destiny comes upon us through normal, everyday moments that connect us to certain people or situations. Moses simply had to respond to the event placed before him and a new door would open up for him.

These seven daughters returned early to their father's tent and told him of the wonderful help Moses had given them. Reuel (Jethro) asked where this man Moses was and found they had left him by the water hole. In a desire to repay Moses with some hospitality he sent his daughters to fetch Moses, inviting him to come, eat and stay with them. Jethro realized very quickly that Moses was an intelligent, gifted man and asked him to stay and become part of his family. Eventually Moses married Zipporah, one of Jethro's daughters.

Jethro was a Midianite priest. The Midianites were nomads who traveled from region to region feeding their flocks. Over the next forty years this Israelite who became an Egyptian was going to cover himself up a second time and become a Midianite. He no longer had a dual personality, he had a triple personality! In other words, the more he ran from his real identity and destiny, the worse his situation became. *But God works all things together for good* (Romans 8:28).

People have often asked me how they can discover their ministry, calling or destiny. I always challenge them to look back and examine their life. By doing this we can see glimpses of it all the way back to our childhood. Our ministry, calling and destiny are, ultimately, an outworking of who we are. They are the very essence of us. People don't go to college and "become" preachers. If you're going to become a preacher you are one already – you go to college to perfect your skills. You can want to be a preacher with all your heart and spend years in the best theological colleges in the world, but if God has not made you to be a preacher, after all that time and expenditure all you will be is a theologically educated non-preacher! God decides what gifts He grants to each person and those gifts reveal themselves from childhood, little by little.

My mother once told my father that she believed when I grew older I would travel the world. At the time I was about three years old! Curious, my father asked why she thought that. Her answer was simple and yet contained profound insight. She told him that whenever we walked past a shop which sold suitcases I screamed and screamed until she let me go play with them. She had perceived something of my future by the way I loved suitcases! But she was absolutely right. At the time of writing this book I have traveled to at least 30 different countries to minister and to some countries on many different occasions.

My father was a talented singer and choir master and he encouraged me to sing. I so loved to sing as a child that my parents entered me for singing contests and many times I gained first place. My mother told stories about how she would often find me dressed up in my best clothes, hair slicked back with my father's Brylcreem, standing in front of her bedroom mirror clutching her hairbrush, singing the latest pop song, totally lost in my little world of entertainment. She used to creep upstairs and spy on me through the crack in the door with a huge smile on her face, watching me go through my "moves". At some point in the performance I would realize she was watching, but I never got embarrassed because I knew she loved to see me dreaming of a great future for myself. She would want to know who I was pretending to be: was it Cliff Richard or Elvis Presley today? I may have been singing their songs, with my hair combed the same way as them, but I didn't dream of being either of them. I dreamt of myself on stage with thousands in the audience enjoying my singing.

Over the years that dream has become more and more fulfilled – though not quite in the way I imagined as a teenage boy. At fourteen years old I picked up the guitar for the first time and began a life of standing in front of crowds entertaining them with my versions of other people's songs or performing my own songs in concerts on radio and television. When I became a Christian the dream was fulfilled even more and since 1977 I've recorded seven worship albums, been involved in thousands of events live and on television, and ministered to millions of people on every continent through my singing and preaching. I don't say any of this to boast, but to show that the "glimpses" of destiny go all the way back to our childhood. I didn't suddenly "become" a singer or a person who could communicate to large audiences – it is intrinsically who I am as a person and time allowed it to be revealed. However much I had dreamed of something like this happening, it would not have come to pass if I'd been tone deaf! This is the problem with so many people. They look at others, see how their lives are making an impact, and want what they have. Instead we must accept who we are and not try to be like anyone else. Then God can help us to be successful in our own way.

"Moses, Moses!" A blast from the past!

Moses had been born into a Jewish family in slavery and poverty. His Jewish beginnings instilled in him the knowledge of God's existence, His power, His sovereignty. He had heard of the way in which God had led and protected Israel since the days of Adam until now. His mother had quietly sung over him daily the songs of Israel. She told him the stories of Adam and Eve, Noah, Abraham, Isaac, Jacob and Joseph. He had a "spiritual" foundation. He understood that God chose people to reveal Himself to, gave them a destiny, and when in trouble they could call on Him for help and He would send a deliverer, a Messiah, a Savior. Buried deep within Moses was the destiny to be that deliverer that Israel were crying out for. He was already among them. God was preparing him for greatness, but it would cost him everything.

Then for almost forty years Moses was raised in Pharaoh's house. He discovered and learned the Egyptian skills of building according to a vision, organization and communication. He learned to be a leader. But he also gained a weakness. He had accomplished all this in his own strength, not God's. The dictator within him must die before God could use him.

Possessions, power, position or people?

Forty more years in the wilderness taught Moses how to be nomadic, wander the wilderness and survive in the harshest of climates. He learned to live without the "things" he once thought were important back in the days when he lived in a palace. He needed to learn there is something much more important than possessions, power and position. He needed to value people. He learned to be a shepherd to someone else's sheep, lead them, feed them, care for and protect them. He was discovering a relationship with God was more precious than anything or anyone.

CHAPTER 5

DEALING WITH THE PAST TO WALK INTO THE FUTURE

Family comes before ministry

For more than thirty years now I have been saved, been a preacher, pastored churches and circled the world as a traveling ministry. In the past ten years I have gone through the toughest and most challenging season of my life. Earlier I recorded how in 1999 my father died, then my mother in 2000 and then my wife, Anne, in 2001. Following on from these tragic events, in 2002, the Lord asked me to relinquish my churches, my position as a leader, my home, my town and even my family – all at a time when I needed them in my life so much. He asked me to step out and trust Him, completely letting go of all I had ever known to lay hold of everything I had ever dreamed of.

I was already rocking and reeling from all that had happened in my life and it was a real challenge to obey Him. My soul wanted desperately to hold onto everything I knew. But I knew I had heard from the Lord, so faith was within my spirit. I stepped out in faith, Heaven opened to me, and doors around the world opened everywhere for me to preach. I was preaching non-stop in great churches and God's power and provision was evident to all. It seemed everything was going so well.

Then, in 2006, everything turned again. Gwenda (my new wife) and I experienced three extremely painful years at the hands of ministries, churches and government bodies. We were lied to, lied about, used and abused. Churches who once chased us, wanting us to minister to them, now totally ignored us and our situation. We had both sold all our possessions to move to the USA in 2006, in obedience to the Lord's call, and had gone to help an international ministry start a Bible college. Now, suddenly, we found ourselves selling all we owned again – but this time to pay our bills and try to keep ourselves and the ministry going. We spent eighteen months living in other people's homes, borrowing their cars, phones and anything else to just survive, many times without a penny or cent in our pockets or bank accounts.

Some presumed we were struggling because of some sin, others because we had disobeyed the Lord. We soul-searched and prayed for many hours, in case we had done anything that was displeasing the Lord, causing Him to get our attention, but He constantly reassured us and encouraged us to keep following and trusting Him, which we did. Our great circle of friends was reduced to just a handful of faithful brothers and sisters who understood our hearts and continually helped us. All the while, Gwenda and I prayed for God's long term direction for our lives, but nothing came. Eventually, however, I began to understand that God *had* spoken to us. All that we were presently experiencing was God's way of showing us that a message He had placed in our hearts was an essential message for the Church worldwide – one that we would spend the rest of our lives proclaiming. Let me explain:

Three years ago Gwenda and I were finishing a session with a group of Bible students we were teaching. We ended by getting everyone to stand in a circle and, with interlocking arms, shout "We're family!" These students, at the end of their studies, would soon be in ministry somewhere around the world, many of them on the world's mission fields where one day in the future they would feel very alone. Our desire for them, while in our care, was to sense that they belonged to a spiritual family and had a "mum and dad" who would be there for them throughout their lives to help and support them.

I had just finished sharing with them that God began with a man (Adam), gave him a wife (Eve) and they gave birth to children. The first thing the Lord said after creating Adam was, *"It is not good that man should be alone"* (Genesis 2:18). We can conclude, therefore, that even though God wanted man to have a great personal relationship with Him, He knew Adam needed a family to bring the best out of him and his life. "Family has to come first before ministry" was the message I wanted these students to grasp. I have always believed that, but here in front of these young men and women I felt a new sense of the power of this truth. I wanted to impart it to them for the duration of the time we were together. Today I realize that *this* is the fundamental message that Gwenda and I must impart to others for the rest of our lives. The Church is a family before it is s a ministry. So often the Church can get caught up in activities which cause it to lose focus, The activities in themselves may be good and worthwhile, but if they cause us to forget the principle, seen from Genesis to Revelation, that God wants us to be His *family*, then they are a distraction from what the New Testament Church is supposed to be. Yes, we're to be His priests, His own special people and His nation (1 Peter 2:9). Yes we're to be His Church, Temple, Body, Bride, Army (see Ephesians). But all of these things without "family" as their foundation will be superficial, cold and functional.

The greatest armies are not those with the greatest weaponry and battle skills, but those whose soldiers are bound together in mutual love and service – those who are prepared to sacrifice their lives for their comrades if demanded. If only the Church could understand this principle! We are engaged in a spiritual war for the souls of billions of people on this planet, yet we are divided by prejudices concerning our doctrine, color, style, insecurities and history. How can we win the war when our armory is impotent because we prefer to be divided over such superficial and petty matters? We must do whatever needs to be done to heal the family, regardless of past history. We can have no prejudice whatsoever in the Church. We are the family of God. A family reflects the father of the house, therefore we must learn to reflect our Heavenly Father. He saves all who call upon His name regardless of sin, gender, color, culture or past history. All are saved by one thing: the blood of Jesus and nothing else. If He is willing to save an individual or an ethnic group and include them in His family, no Christian or church can argue with it. We must accept everyone who calls Christ Savior.

More than that, if we say we truly love God we must go to our enemies and put our differences right and, as far as it is possible, forgive them and love them with His unconditional love to win them into His family. We must take His Gospel even to those who have hurt us the most, because we have no prejudice. What a witness it would be to see Christians from Israel ministering to people in or from Germany or vice versa. How incredibly powerful the message would be to see American Christian missionaries giving their lives to take His love to the people of Iran, Iraq or Afghanistan. That would reveal the love of God. No one is converted simply by a message about God's love for them, but by a *demonstration* of His love for them.

Church growth experts tell us that there are more people who used to be active members of a church and no longer attend, than there are current members of churches. Sadly, we have labeled them as "backsliders" instead of trying to understand what is going on in their lives and helping them. Over half of our known "family" is missing, wounded in action, yet we, their brothers and sisters, are doing precious little to bring them home. We spend millions in finance and manpower to share the Gospel through literature and terrestrial and online media, presenting a view of the Church that is glorious and successful, while neglecting the most effective way to bring people to Christ. Jesus' mandate that, *"By this love will all men know you are my disciples"* does not seem to motivate many in the Church. The world is crying out to be loved and accepted and the Church is trying to preach at them and be God's spiritual police force in the earth, making sure everyone lives right. Yet, we cannot fulfill the greatest commission to love one another, our own "family", let alone the people of the world.

People catch what you've got, not what you say you've got

The truth is: you cannot give what you don't have. If I have measles then you won't catch chicken pox from me – you can only catch what I have! If I am filled with God's love and it directs the way I live, then people will catch it from me. If I profess to have God's love when I really don't, then no one will be affected by it. If I possess God's kind of love, that is unconditional and free from prejudice, accepting others as they are, then I must first have received this from God as a revelation for myself. The more I am persuaded that God accepts me with His unconditional love, the more it will affect me and the more I will take on His likeness. Consequently, the more I become like Him, the more His likeness will be channeled through me to touch others.

When the Church is divided, does not act like one family and does not bring home the "prodigals" it reveals where our real problem lies: in our personal relationship with God, our heavenly Father. We must allow Him to work in our hearts and understanding. We must catch His Spirit, have His desires, see everyone and everything from His perspective and be motivated by what motivates Him. Surely the birth, life, death and resurrection of Jesus conveys that His kind of love reaches, rescues and restores lives, while He pays for it all Himself. His whole motivation and purpose is bring back His lost family. But is it ours?

Outside the "camp" believers

Moses was alone in the wilderness. He no longer belonged to Israel's or Egypt's camp. He didn't feel like he belonged anywhere, in fact, and that can easily lead a person to think they have blown it with God. But sometimes God has to bring His people out of the "camps" they've been in (i.e. streams or denominations) to teach them that which they could never learn whilst inside them.

Christians today can be pretty scathing about any brother or sister who doesn't automatically believe what their pastor, stream or denomination believes. In fact, I am now more aware than any other time in my Christian life just how many of God's people no longer desire to be pigeon-holed into one camp or another. As a result they have moved outside the walls and barriers that churches erect, allegedly to "protect" their sheep from harm, but which, in reality, segregate the body of Christ. These "outside the camp" believers have seen something new and want to be part of it. It's called the "kingdom of God" perspective. Not all of these renegades are outside God's will for their lives or in sin, despite disrespectfully being called backsliders. If anything, they have been awakened to the foundational truth that there is a life that cannot be found in church meetings, but only when you are alone with God.

Church leaders were never meant to make Christians dependent upon their preaching, teaching, guidance and counseling. We are meant to teach people to know God personally, to open the Word and understand it for themselves with the purpose of teaching others. Every Christian is meant to learn to hear God for themselves and trust His guidance for their lives. I am not saying we don't need teachers, preachers or counselors, but we shouldn't want or need them more than we need Jesus. Sometimes the only way the Lord can accomplish this in your life is to take you outside the camp to meet with Him in a new way, which is what He did with Moses, isolating him while He dealt with every scar, every bit of unforgiveness, pain, resentment and prejudice he carried in his heart against anyone from any culture. Moses was being prepared not just to be the deliverer of Israel, but all people who needed and wanted to be free from slavery and bondage. He must come to love all. Every Christian ministry must learn this lesson. God is the Savior, Deliverer, Redeemer, Healer, Restorer and Lover of all. He has no prejudice or desire to segregate people.

Moses, the Israelite/Egyptian/Midianite had to die. He was about to encounter God in a burning bush in the backside of the desert, alone. One Moses had entered the wilderness, but another Moses would emerge from it. Just as he buried an Egyptian in the sand to cover up his sin, so God was going to "bury" the old Moses. Out of this wilderness would come a man sent of God with a new heart, a new spirit and a new mindset. He would walk in his calling as a deliverer, not wanting anyone to perish, wanting to impart to everyone the grace he himself had experienced.

Moses would need all the skills he had learned over eighty years for the task God had prepared for him. But the greatest lessons he would learn in the wilderness would be to love and serve God more than people, to be himself not what others wanted or needed him to be, and to allow God to free him from fear, failure, pain and prejudice. But first Moses had to be emptied of himself. He had to let go of everything he had ever known to lay hold of everything he had ever dreamed of. So must you and I in order to live the life of abundance Jesus offers us.

A new perspective on life

Jesus said in John 10:10,

"The thief does not come except to steal, and to kill, and to

destroy. I have come that they may have life, and that they may have it more abundantly."

The "thief" had certainly worked on Moses during his eighty years and he had wandered as far away from his roots and family as was possible. We find him in the furthest regions of the wilderness, feeling far from God and the destiny he dreamed of as a small child. But he is about to have a pivotal encounter and in one moment everything in his world will be turned upside down by God.

"Now Moses was tending the flock of Jethro his father-in-law, the priest of Midian. And he led the flock to the back of the desert, and came to Horeb, the mountain of God. And the Angel of the Lord appeared to him in a flame of fire from the midst of a bush. So he looked, and behold, the bush was burning with fire, but the bush was not consumed. Then Moses said, 'I will now turn aside and see this great sight, why the bush does not burn.'

So when the Lord saw that he turned aside to look, God called to him from the midst of the bush and said, 'Moses, Moses!'

And he said, 'Here I am.'

Then He said, 'Do not draw near this place. Take your sandals off your feet, for the place where you stand is holy ground.' Moreover He said, 'I am the God of your father—the God of Abraham, the God of Isaac, and the God of Jacob.' And Moses hid his face, for he was afraid to look upon God.

And the Lord said: 'I have surely seen the oppression of My people who are in Egypt, and have heard their cry because of their taskmasters, for I know their sorrows. So I have come down to deliver them out of the hand of the Egyptians, and to bring them up from that land to a good and large land, to a land flowing with milk and honey, to the place of the Canaanites and the Hittites and the Amorites and the Perizzites and the Hivites and the Jebusites. Now therefore, behold, the cry of the children of Israel has come to Me, and I have also seen the oppression with which the Egyptians oppress them. Come now, therefore, and I will send you to Pharaoh that you may bring My people, the children of Israel, out of Egypt.'

But Moses said to God, 'Who am I that I should go to Pharaoh, and that I should bring the children of Israel out of Egypt?'" (Exodus 3:1-11)

At this point we need to fully grasp the intricate details of the words laid before us, so that we fully appreciate all that is happening in this encounter with God and his lost son, Moses. It is approximately eighty years since Moses was born, initially hidden away in his parent's home before being cast into the Nile in a basket. It is forty years since his abortive attempt at being a deliver for the Israelites forced him to flee into the wilderness. Since then he has wandered the desert as a shepherd. The early prophesies over his life seem a distant memory and dream now. Moses is old, his natural youth and ability gone. He is sure that he has failed in life so badly that it is impossible for his dreams to be fulfilled. He has also wandered away from God, but is about to discover that when we feel furthest from the Lord, often we are the closest to Him. Let's take a closer look:

"What Is that in your hand?"

The opening verses of Exodus chapter 4 describe Moses standing with a staff in his hand. It sounds perfectly normal for a shepherd to be holding a staff, but this was no ordinary staff. Remember that Moses would be the person who, in his final forty years as the leader of God's people, would write the first five books of the Bible. In Genesis he recorded the complete account of Creation, Adam and Eve, the events that led to Israel ending up in Egypt as slaves and everything in between. He was a chronologist. This history was not transcribed on paper originally, but carved into stones, painted on walls and, more usually, carved carefully onto a wooden staff that was passed from generation to generation so that people understood the genealogy of their forefathers and the major events of their history. Each new generation would inscribe onto the staff their own part of this history and chronology for future generations. Moses, therefore, was leaning on his history. In his hand was the evidence of God's miraculous ways in dealing with His people. One glance would have reminded Moses that being eighty years old was nothing, since etched onto that staff were the names of Abraham and Sarah, his ancestors who gave birth to a son when 100 and 99 years old respectively.

If Moses felt ashamed of his past failure, underneath his grasp was the reminder that Adam and Eve failed God and sinned in the beginning. He possessed in his hand the account of Noah getting drunk, of Jacob deceiving his own father to gain the blessing reserved for his older brother. If he still struggled with issues of rejection, all he needed was to look to the story of Joseph's rejection, being sold into slavery by his own brothers who hated him. Everything Moses had experienced or was currently going through had been experienced by others before him. A second glance would have helped him see that God used every one of those so-called failures to impact their world. If God could do it with them, He could do it with Moses, regardless of his age or past events. In his hand was everything he needed to encourage his faith, but he still couldn't see it. So, God had to change Moses' viewpoint and, if necessary, He will do the same with us.

Moses thought he was far from God and that God had probably abandoned him. Nothing could have been further from the truth. He was about to discover God was with him in his darkest, lowest moment. He had God behind him (Mount Horeb, the "Mount of God") and God in front of him (the burning bush). God had hemmed Moses in to confront this lost, defeated son of His. He will do the same with you and me whenever necessary.

Moses heard the crackling of wood and, turning towards the

sound, saw a bush on fire. This in itself was not a strange sight – bushes often spontaneously combusted in the heat of the Sinai Desert – so he ignored it. But the sound of crackling wood continued until Moses turned to look once again, wondering how long this bush could keep burning. He discovered to his astonishment that though the bush was engulfed in flames, the wood was not consumed. This was different and it got his attention. He rose from the rock he was resting on and slowly walked towards this amazing sight. Moses had been looking in the wrong direction. He had viewed everything that had taken place in his life as a failure, not as preparation for the greatest deliverance in history. But in one moment the Lord had intervened with something unfamiliar, unexpected, turned his head, and his view had changed. Instead of standing motionless, leaning heavily on his staff, looking in the wrong direction, God had turned him around and now he was moving towards the bush that was on fire and full of God's presence. At last he was moving towards God!

Deep calls unto deep

God in His infinite mercy and grace recognizes our times of weakness and knows that there are times in our lives when we feel "lost" to all that we believed, hoped or dreamed of earlier in our lives. It's not that we doubt God's ability or His word – it is more that we question how much of what we dreamed, or was prophesied over our lives, was pure fantasy and wishful thinking. We begin to doubt *our* ability to hear from Him or discern His word correctly. It is at this point He lovingly begins the process of gaining our attention afresh by intervening in our lives in the most unexpected way. He uses what we least expect to gain our attention.

From childhood Moses knew of the prophesy spoken over his life. For years he had pondered those words, wondering how and when it would happen, if it would happen in the way he thought. He had seen the slavery of Israel grow more and more unbearable and it was intolerable for him to watch. He had also seen what had happened the moment he tried to step into the role of the "deliverer", so desperately needed by his people. Painfully and tragically he had discovered that it is one thing to have the word of God spoken over your life and the gifting to fulfill it, but another thing entirely to understand God's grace and timing for its fulfillment. Prophets and leaders must learn not only to know *what* God desires to do, but also *how* and *when* He desires to do it. I teach that God's *mission* must be done through his *man* (or woman) who has His *message* using His *method* at His *moment* to the correct *multitude*. (I elaborate on his in my book *Alignment for Assignment*). It is never enough just to have the word. The man and the message have to be the same! It had taken eighty years, but finally Moses was coming into alignment – he was beginning to "fit" the message God wanted him to deliver.

Notice that it was only when Moses was up and moving towards the bush that God spoke to him. He didn't speak while Moses was sitting still. Challenging events, offences and confusing situations are all tests to see if we will stop moving towards God's promises and prophesies. Everyone in the Bible who had great prophetic words and promises given to them endured such testing times when they could easily have given up and said, "I can't take any more!" But great miracles come in the moment of extreme testing of our faith, when we refuse to let go of the promises of God, not matter how much it costs us or what is the outcome. If you have been knocked down or out of the race, let me encourage you that the Lord is trying to get you moving again and the first place to go is in the right direction: towards Him!

Moses was moving closer to God and closer to that pivotal moment when his life would change – and not only his, but the lives of a nation. "Moses, Moses!" called the voice from the bush.

He was being confronted with God in a way that he'd never heard of before and was completely outside his knowledge and understanding. How did Moses react? How would we have reacted? I think I would have fallen down with fear and shock. I don't imagine Moses took this event lightly and reacted casually – his mind must have been racing at a million miles per second as he tried to process what was happening. It wasn't possible for a bush to speak – and it knew his Egyptian name! Surely this was God, but why would He appear now, after all these years?

Although petrified, each time the voice called his name it resonated deep within his soul. It hurt him. He wanted to react by backing away, withdrawing to some place of safety where he could hear the voice no more. Yet, at the same time he was desperate to hear God's voice and, for once, resisted the temptation to run. Deep down he knew that when God confronts you, *you can run but you just can't hide.*

Today you may be at a similar place in your life, wanting to run from God instead of towards him. Maybe I can help you. When you would rather run from God than towards Him, when you have failed or you are in pain because of someone or something, then you need to understand your perception of God is wrong. When everyone, including yourself, has let you down or brought pain into your life, He is not the one to run from. He is the one to run to because He will never fail you, nor will His unconditional love towards you ever cease. He expressed that love for you by allowing His Son, Jesus, to die the most horrendous death on a cross at Calvary – the same love that He has for you when everything is seemingly going wrong in your life. He is the one stable, reliable person you can turn to in the deepest, darkest moments of your life because He is faithful.

God can speak to you and reveal Himself at the most unusual times and in the most unusual ways, but His voice and His word will always be involved and evident. He cannot contradict His Word, the Bible. It is His Word, His oath. He and His Word are one and the same.

The Lord gave this man the name "Moses" on purpose. It means "drawn out one" or to pull out, to draw out as water (Strong's H4871), just as Moses was drawn out of the Nile by Pharaoh's daughter. Moses knew instinctively that God the Father was reaching all the way back into his earliest days to remind him that he was drawn out of his mothers womb, drawn out of the River Nile, drawn out of Pharaoh's house, drawn out of Egypt into the wilderness, drawn out of the Midianite camp in order for God to draw out of him every bit of pain, disillusionment, offence, disappointment, discouragement, fear and guilt of the past. God did this so He could send Moses back into those very places and people groups to draw them out of their bondage and slavery and draw them back into the promises of God, that they might inherit all of God's wonderful love and provision for their lives. This was going to be one painful event for Moses, for he was being asked to trust God again when all he had gone through had taught him to not trust anyone but himself. He knew it would be painful to let go and trust God with his life again, but it was infinitely better than slowly dying within, feeling lost, wondering what the meaning of his life was. No doubt the deep seated emotions that Moses had suppressed for years came tumbling out at that moment. God's love and presence have an incredible ability to do that to us at such moments. Although a proud man by nature, Moses bent his head, grasping his staff in both hands to prop himself up as he found it hard to keep standing throughout this encounter.

What goes in must come out

When God designed and formed Adam he placed an opening at the top of his body called a mouth through which he could receive food and an exit at the other end to let out the refuse, which in the UK we call our backside! In between He fashioned an intricate digestive system that broke down the food, absorbed the nutrients turned them into energy, and jettisoned the waste products. Nutritionists tell us that food needs to pass quickly through our digestive systems and the waste must not remain in our bodies as ultimately it will poison us. Our natural bodies teach us a spiritual truth: all we take into our lives that has the potential to poison our souls must be flushed out by God's grace. If we try to hang onto those things, we will become sick and they will begin to destroy us from the inside out.

Moses had come to this place – the "backside" of the desert – to receive such a divine colonic irrigation! All that had stunted and crippled his spiritual development, keeping him walking around in circles in the wilderness for forty years, was flushed out of his spirit and soul. Today, allow God to similarly cleanse you of the garbage of the past. Don't let past failure do the same to you as it did to Moses.

CHAPTER 6

IT'S OKAY TO BE WHO I AM

Quietly Moses spoke to God. His first words were, "Here I am." Did Moses really believe he could get away with that? Did he really think a simple statement like this was enough to deal with everything on God's agenda? Just like Adam in the garden who told God, "Here I am", but had actually covered himself with fig-leaves to hide his nakedness, so Moses had deceived himself. He didn't realize the depth of *truth* being demanded of him by God.

Jesus once said to His disciples,

*"You shall know the **truth**, and the **truth** shall make you free."* (John 8:32)

When talking with the woman at the well Jesus said to her,

*"God is Spirit, and those who worship Him must worship in spirit and **truth**."* (John 4:24)

The Greek word for "truth" used here in the Bible means "liberated, delivered, a citizen … no longer a slave to someone or something, exempt from obligation, a free man or woman" (Strongs 1659). God wanted to set Moses free and in order to do that, they had to get to grips with the truth. Moses was being confronted with an issue God has to address with us all: in order for Him to do what He wants to do in our life, we must come to the clear knowledge of who we really are and accept that God loves us precisely as we are. Tragically most people, without

God's intervention, never fully come to this place of self-discovery. Moses had no clue who he really was. In fact, he was more confused about it now than at any point in his life. He was a Jew, covered by an Egyptian, who had been buried underneath a Midianite! But God was calling him out. Which Moses did God want to meet?

Moses was blind to the depth of his problem. To help him out God asked him to do something. Most people don't fully appreciate its significance:

"Moses, take your sandals off your feet, for the place where you stand is holy ground." (Exodus 3:5)

To Western readers this can sound a little odd, but in many nations it is culturally acceptable, and expected, that when you enter a place of worship or someone's house you slip off your shoes and walk around in your bare feet, socks, or in slippers provided by the host.

Some preachers say this act was symbolic of God inviting Moses to step into *His house* in the midst of this wilderness and, of course, there would be lessons we could learn from that. Another theologian pointed out to me once that shoes "elevate" us a little. So the removal of Moses' sandals represented him "lowering" himself i.e. humbling himself before God. It is true that all pride has to be removed if we desire to have fellowship with Him. Once again, there is merit in this illustration. But it is neither of these insights that grip my heart as I read the account of God confronting Moses.

After reading this passage of Scripture many times I prayed that God would reveal to me the deeper understanding that I sensed existed in the text. I could not immediately "see" it with my natural understanding, but it would be revealed in due course –

during a trip to Mexico!

You're standing in a holy place

Early in the 1990's I traveled with friends from the USA into Mexico to preach for a weekend. On the Monday morning, as we were saying our farewells to the pastor and his team, someone asked if we had ever seen the sea along the Mexican Gulf. I replied we had not and so they suggested that instead of taking the straight route back to San Antonio where we had come from, we would travel due East, straight for the ocean, and afterwards make our way back to Texas. We agreed and followed their advice, looking forward to seeing "the most beautiful coast, beaches and sea you've ever seen." It took several hours but eventually we arrived, driving our vehicles up onto a grass bank that overlooked a beach. The pastor was right! We got out of our cars totally stunned by the beautiful scene. Someone asked if we had time to stop for a swim and I said yes. At this point, the big kid in me took over and I began to take off my T-shirt, throw aside my sandals and run down the bank onto the beach shouting, "Last one in buys lunch!" My friends shouted that I was cheating as they too began stripping off, rushing towards the sand in their bathing trunks, eagerly anticipating swimming in the warm waters of the Gulf of Mexico.

My friends stopped suddenly, however, as they heard me screaming and watched with amusement as I ran around on the sand. I was hopping, skipping, turning around, and running back to the grass as fast as I could, at the same time frantically trying to brush the sand from the soles of my feet, yelling, "It's hot! It's burning!" Of course, they fell about laughing, wondering what on earth I was on about. "What's burning your feet?" one called over. "The sand, of course!" I replied. They were amazed. We were all from Wales where the sand never gets hot. But here in Mexico, the sand was scalding!

As I sat on the grass brushing sand off my feet, looking for my sandals, the Lord spoke to me very clearly and suddenly gave me insight into those verses about Moses. He said, "If it's this hot in Mexico, how hot would it have been in Sinai, the hottest desert in the world?" As those words dropped into my spirit all I could think of was God asking Moses to take off his sandals. Moses would have known how hot the sand was in the heat of the day. Sheer self-preservation would have challenged God's request as folly. So God asked him again. Moses must have replied telling God what He already knew: "It will be blisteringly hot! It'll take the skin off my feet! It'll hurt!" All of these things God already knew, yet He still asked Moses to obey Him. Moses' objections had not changed God's mind. The real Moses was "covered over" and God's desire was to uncover him in order for him to move on. This was what God really wanted to see: Moses' unmasked and surrendered.

God had to make Moses vulnerable in order to "strip away" all his self-sufficiency and the baggage of the past. Let's look at this process God executes in our lives from a different perspective by fast-forwarding forty years to the time just after Moses has said goodbye to Israel and climbed a mountain to die, leaving Joshua, his disciple, to be the national leader and take the people into Canaan, the Promised Land.

Transition Is preceded by a stripping away

"Moses My servant is dead. Now therefore arise, go over this Jordon, you and all the people, to the land I am giving them ..." are the first words Joshua heard from God and conveyed to the people as their new leader (Joshua 1:2). Joshua obeyed and once they had made camp (Joshua 5:1-12) we read that once again God speaks to Joshua saying, *"Make flint knives for yourself and circumcise the sons of Israel"* (v2).

Picture this event now as if you were there, witnessing the scene for yourself. Read between the lines of this account and imagine what must have taken place. Joshua did not just hear God's voice, go and make some flint knives and hurriedly circumcise everyone with no problem. Here's what I think must have happened:

Joshua heard the instruction of God to circumcise all the men of Israel and was willing to obey, but he didn't have the tools to do the job. God told him to use flint knives, so that's what he'd do. But how many would he need? One historian has estimated there were some 600,000 men in the camp. They were going to need a lot of priests with a lot of knives to remove a lot of foreskins! It was going to be quite some time before every man bore this sign of God's covenant. Just as the priests needed time to prepare flint knives and carry out the task, so God takes His time to prepare us and bring us to the place where it is obvious for all to see that we are His covenant people.

Eventually the 600,000 were called together for a "men's meeting" with Pastor Joshua! They had great respect for their leader and had heard that God had recently spoken to him. They were all excited to hear God's word to them at this time. They had no idea what was coming next! Stay with me now, and please don't be offended as I further unpack this event in graphic terms. If we read this short text casually we miss so much meaning. But if we look closer at what happens when a man is circumcised we see an amazing truth highlighted about how God sets us free and sets us apart to be used by Him. It is actually incredibly funny (if you have a sense of humor like me, that is!)

Joshua stood on the edge of a mountain so as to be in full view of all the men. Either side of him stood the new co-leaders of Israel, all born in the wilderness. The only living survivors of Egypt were Joshua himself and Caleb. Priests had lined up either side as well and the 600,000 men stood in ranks facing Joshua. At this point

Joshua explains that he has been in prayer, asking the Lord for the strategy needed to take the land ahead of them. This is such a normal thing for a leader to do, even today. Churches all over the world are seeking the Lord for the key strategies that will enable them to evangelize the nations they live in. Every leader must, therefore, learn what Joshua learnt. He announces, "Men, I have the word of the Lord regarding how to take the land …" The atmosphere is electric with anticipation. Men with clenched fists up and down the ranks shout out "Yes!" in excitement. They were up for a battle. The confinement of the wilderness has done its job: they would do *anything* to leave it behind and move on (which is the place we all come to before we can break free of our past and enter into all God has for us). "The word of the Lord is," Joshua continues, "Be ye circumcised!"

Ha! The men were deliriously happy. God had spoken! But wait a minute … one by one they looked at each other in confusion. What did Joshua just say? We have to be *circumcised?* What does that mean? The majority had no idea what circumcision was! One man called to an older friend in his line, "Abe, what's circumcision?" Abe tried to explain what he had heard about it, but everyone around him laughed. "No, no, he asked what *circumcision* was. What are you talking about?" Patient Abe told them again what he believed was about to happen, at which point Joshua cried out, "Priests, forward march" and the sound of thousands of priests approaching the men, sharpening their flint knives changed the mood from jubilation to panic. Could God really be asking them to do something so embarrassingly painful as this?

As the priests arrived at the first line of soldiers you can imagine the men turning to each other saying, "You go first!" "No way, after you!" No one wanted to be the first to be circumcised. Everyone wanted the priests to "practice" on someone else before it was their turn! After all, the priests had never circumcised anyone in their lives.

Imagine the vulnerability this produced in the men. They were being asked to reveal the most intimate, private part of their anatomy. "What if the priest makes a mistake? One slip of the knife could ruin my manhood!" Imagine having to suddenly place your manhood in another man's hands, especially one wielding a sharp instrument. Each man had to become vulnerable as never before and endure a painful experience, the mark of which he would bear for the rest of his life.

Each priest cut a circle of flesh away from the top of each man's penis. The foreskin of a man who has never been circumcised is covering the glans or "head" underneath in order to protect it, because it is the most sensitive part of a man's anatomy. The tearing away of the foreskin, exposing the glans caused excruciating pain – there was no such thing as a local anesthetic! The agony on the face of every man was clear to see. But despite the horrible pain that was involved, something was now revealed in the life of each man that had remained covered all his life. The clear message from God was this: there can be no covering up of your tenderness and vulnerability. The place of intimacy must be revealed. There may be some pain involved in getting there, but God wants to released us into a new transparency in our relationship with Him and others. God desires His people to be intimate with Him. There can be no covering up.

In a place of completely trusting God to protect you

Reading the narrative in the book of Joshua, we discover that at this very moment Israel's enemies were encamped on the mountains overlooking the whole event. Six hundred thousand men were bent over in pain, gingerly hobbling around the camp praying their enemies would not attack, because they were in no fit state to fight a battle. And this is the very point of the whole account. God brings us to a place of incredible intimacy with Him, but He also requires us to learn to live in a place of great vulnerability and dependency upon Him. Notice that while Israel were in this place of vulnerability God kept their enemies at bay.

So often, we try to work out our lives in our own power and strength. We are afraid of real intimacy and transparency with God, but it is the foundational need of every man and woman of God.

Look at this passage from Genesis chapter 2:

*"And the Lord God said, 'It is not good that man should be **alone;** I will make him a helper comparable to him.' ... And the Lord God caused a deep sleep to fall on Adam, and he slept; and He took one of his ribs, and closed up the flesh in its place. Then the rib which the Lord God had **taken from man** He made into a woman, and He brought her to the man."* (Genesis 2:18-22)

The word "alone" used in this passage means "separate, divided, solitary". A modern word frequently used to describe being alone or solitary is "disconnected". Men in particular are good at being disconnected. We tend to have an "external me" and an "internal me", so that it's not always easy to really get to know us. Notice God took something "out of" Adam and fashioned Eve with it. He was the *external*, she was the *internal*. Isn't this how it is? Men are much more externally-minded than women. Women don't need coercing to share their feelings and express their emotions. But men frequently find it hard to express themselves and share their heart.

Most men easily live a life of cover-up. They present one image, but on the inside is a whole other world they never reveal due to the fear of rejection. But men are weakened because of living this way and God wants to hold up a mirror to our lives so that we see ourselves as we really are and break free from that bondage. All our covering up does nothing to impresses God and it does not help us.

Power is released through intimacy
– the walls came down!

Immediately after the soldiers had received their circumcision the Lord commanded them to march around the city of Jericho, whose walls were apparently so wide that three chariots could race around the top of them side by side. Israel was to do this for six days remaining silent throughout. On the seventh day they were to circle the city seven times, concluding with one almighty roar of praise to God. When they did this the walls of Jericho collapsed completely. Jericho was a huge city, with a huge defense system, yet the consecrating act of circumcision had released a new sound, a new level of praise so great that it broke down the very molecular structure of the stone and turned it to dust before them. The work of circumcision had placed Israel in a position to receive this great miracle and their enemy was defeated.

The men had gone around in circles before a shout was released and the walls of cover-up and protection were removed, allowing Israel to step into a new level of victory and receive a portion of the Land of Promise. Do we see the spiritual dynamic here behind the physical event? As we walk with God and one another in intimacy and truth, it positions us to receive God's powerful grace, and this enables us to become who we're meant to become. It allows us to have what we're supposed to have and to do what we're supposed to do.

To complete this lesson we need to look at one more event: what happened when Israel tried to capture Ai (Joshua 7). Their plans failed because one man, Achan, had taken some of the treasure of Jericho – which God had forbidden them to take. Everything in

Jericho was supposed to be razed to the ground, "devoted" to God as an offering as His people entered the land, but Achan stole some treasure and buried it in the sand beneath his tent, covering it over. This was the very opposite of what circumcision had taught them. Every man had experienced this painful lesson so that God would have a people who walked in intimacy and transparency. But one man had returned to a life of covering up. As a result, thirty-six of his countrymen died in Israel's defeat. How important and powerful it is for us to remain in a place of intimate, vulnerable worship as we walk with God.

But who am I?

Let's return now to Moses at the burning bush. He slipped off his sandals in response to the Lord's request and placed his feet on the sand, each grain burning into his skin, feeling like the point of a needle. Unable to keep his feet stationary Moses lifted one foot after the other, trying to alleviate the scalding heat of the sand, but God wanted both his feet planted firmly on the ground. Gradually, Moses stood slowly, soles burning, tears stinging his eyes. We must endure God's dealings with us until the desire to flee or cover ourselves up ceases and we can stand before Him naked and unashamed, knowing His love for us is more reliable than our love for ourselves.

At the beginning of this encounter with God Moses had said, "Here I am." Now, standing motionless before God, he hears his commission. He is going back to Egypt in the power of God to bring the entire nation out of slavery to Pharaoh. At the same time God will destroy Pharaoh forever. God was going to do it, not Moses. He didn't want Moses' strength, strategies or so-called wisdom. He only wanted a willing worshipper, one who loved to spend time alone with Him. God was looking for someone who would love Him more than people, one who would fear Him more than people, situations or enemies. This is still what God desires.

Moses' response at the end of this is, "Who am I?" (Exodus 3:11). The whole process had exposed the fact that he did not know who he really was. Moses had been on the run for so many years and buried himself under so many cultures and traditions that he didn't have a clue who he was. But in one moment God confronted all his issues, delivered him from the guilt and fear of the past, changed his perception of God and himself, and set him free to be the person God had always intended him to be.

It's okay to be yourself before God, no matter what others in your "camp" may say. You will only rise to your full potential when you allow God to break you free from being a slave to the opinions, needs or traditions of others. We can only bring others into the level of freedom we ourselves have experienced. If we're not free, we won't be able to set anyone else free. Remember that people will only "catch what we've got, not what we say we've got". We cannot give a person something we do not have. We cannot guide people where we have never been. This is precisely why God took Moses into the wilderness to learn how to live there for forty years before sending him back to liberate Israel. Though Moses could not see God's hand upon his life in the wilderness, God had been with him, preparing him for a great destiny.

There is one more biblical character we need to learn from in our journey. In the next chapter we examine how God led Elijah through a similar encounter.

CHAPTER 7

RAVEN'S FOOD

1 Kings 17:1 introduces us to Elijah, an unknown prophet of God, who appears on the scene out of the wilderness at a time when evil King Ahab is on the throne. Ahab was a wicked man with an even more wicked wife, Jezebel. Between them they had turned the people completely away from God to worship idols and false gods. Therefore God appoints a man who will do His will and turn the nation back to Him.

Elijah brings the prophetic word of the Lord to Ahab and declares, with great boldness, that a drought is coming upon the land that will continue as long as he says so. What audacity! A totally unheard of prophet speaks to a king like this, seemingly unaware that the king could cut him down in a second. Some preparation must have occurred in this young man's life for him to be willing and able to handle such a commission. Indeed, Elijah had been prepared and God also had further work to do in the life of his servant. How God deals with him gives us an important glimpse into how God prepares all His great ministries for great tasks. We've just examined how God prepared Moses in the wilderness by emptying him of his natural resources and forcing him to depend on the Lord. Now we see God doing a similar thing with this new prophet of His who desires to be used to change his world for good.

Elijah, once he has delivered God's edict to king Ahab, is led by the Holy Spirit to the edge of the wilderness and the Brook Cherith. Here God promises ravens will deliver his breakfast and supper each day, while his water will be provided by the brook.

Let's examine the deeper message in this story.

Transition happens when you accept what you never accepted before

According to the Law of Moses, Ravens were "unclean" birds. God's people were not to eat or even touch them. But here is the God who issued that decree to Moses, telling His servant Elijah that His provision for him in the wilderness will come via something the Law calls unclean. Why would God ask Elijah to violate the Law? Why would God contradict His own command?

Ravens are scavengers by nature. In other words, they wouldn't turn up to feed Elijah each day with nice, freshly sliced meat in their beaks – and there were no supermarkets en route to the Brook Cherith! The birds would be feeding on the dead carcasses of rotting animals left in a field somewhere and they would be regurgitating that meat onto a rock in front of Elijah. Do you get the picture?

Elijah was no different to you or me. He sat by the brook wondering how God was going to accomplish this miracle of provision He had promised in the midst of a nationwide economic recession (drought and famine in biblical language). Suddenly several large ravens appeared in front of him. One by one they "coughed up" regurgitated meat onto the rock and left it there. As Elijah watched, it dawned on him that these were God's waiters in the wilderness – he was being invited to dine upon God's provision. It wasn't exactly what he'd expected or desired. How could he eat such revolting looking, foul smelling and tasting food? "Eat, Elijah" came the voice of God. But Elijah could not. He couldn't get past what he could see with his eyes, smell with his nose and anticipate the taste of with his taste buds! Choked up food from unclean animals? It was a desperate situation. Elijah just couldn't get past the barrier of his thoughts and senses to receive what God was offering. But this is the point of the whole episode.

God needed to help His prophet overcome his narrow minded theological perspectives, his natural thought patterns, and help him stop living based on his senses. God's will and miraculous provision will come to us too, after we learn this same, vital lesson. "Raven's Food" was God's will for Elijah – not to harm him, but to help him reach a place where he would receive greater miracles in his life than he'd ever received before. He was going to have to learn to digest God's meat (His Word), even though it seemed impossible for him to do at this moment. But here is a great truth: *transition happens when you accept what you never accepted before.*

It's amazing how powerful hunger can be. If we are hungry enough, those things we never dreamt of eating or drinking, we will end up eating and drinking! Each day the ravens came with "fresh" food for Elijah and each day he rejected it, only drinking from the brook. The hungrier he became, the more tempted he was to eat the meat, though the thought of it was still abhorrent to him. He even picked it up, sniffed it and placed a small piece in his mouth before spitting it out and washing the taste away with water. But there came a point in Elijah's life, as there will in ours, where God persuaded him to accept His will, no matter how unpalatable it initially seemed.

Elijah got past the barrier of his thoughts and senses and ate the raven's food. He didn't like it, but he ate it. Next time the birds came he ate again, and again after that, each time hating it. But time changes things. Eventually Elijah learned to eat the food without a thought. It shows how God can bring us to a place of acceptance, even though His will at first seemed a bitter experience. In the end, God does this by instilling in us a *hunger* for Him that transcends everything else. For our nations to change and for His miracles to flow once again in our lives and families, we must have this hunger; we must be changed inwardly by His will and His Word to accept what we have not been willing to accept before.

My first personal raven's food encounter

When I was a very new Christian a friend of mind came to see me to encourage me with God's Word. During the course of our conversation he asked me if anyone had taught me what the Bible says about the subject of tithing. I told him that not only had no one taught me, I had never even heard of it! So my friend, Chris, proceeded to walk me through the Scriptures. God's will for my life, he explained, was to give ten percent of my monthly income into His kingdom and God would make the remaining ninety percent go further than the one hundred percent had gone before.

My initial reaction was that I thought he was crazy. I looked at him in utter disbelief, wondering how on earth he could suggest such a thing when he knew full well that my family were struggling terribly financially and getting deeper into debt every month. Unfortunately for Chris, I vented the full force of my feelings on him and frog marched him out of the house, slamming the door after him and muttering that the man was not in his right mind.

But just at that moment, I heard God's voice speak to me very clearly. He asked me whether tithing was in His Word. Of course it was, I acknowledged, I had just read it! He gently showed me that if it was in His Word, then it was His will. He said nothing further to me. Later that month, things became so bad for us financially that we stood on the edge of losing our home. But when I received my monthly salary check I knew exactly what I needed to do. I wrote out a check to cover my tithe, with my heart pounding and my head telling me, "This is not logical!" Under my breath I constantly repeated to myself, *"It is written man shall not live on bread alone, but by every word that proceeds from the mouth of God"* (Matthew 4:4). I knew that God had spoken to me and He never lies and He never breaks a promise.

The next Sunday as the offering basket came around I placed my envelope onto it, every fiber of my being afraid of what I was doing. This act of "foolishness", as I saw it, would probably mean we had no food or cigarette money for the rest of the month. I was literally shaking, but I did it, trusting in the God who does miracles to do one for me. As I let go of that check into the offering basket, a sudden and deep joy erupted within me. It felt so good. Every concern left me instantly.

As the service finished, I went to collect my young son, Matthew, from the children's ministry room. As I ran up the stairs, with shoulders lighter than when I came into the building just a few hours earlier, I passed David, my brother-in law, coming down the stairs. He hastily grabbed hold of me to stop me rushing past him, pulled out his wallet and put some money in my hand. I looked down and there was more money than I had just placed in the offering. "What's this?" I queried, quite stunned. He reminded me that month's ago I'd loaned him some money and he had completely forgotten to pay me back. He said that God had woken him up in the night and reminded him to give it to me – with added interest! I stood there wanting to laugh and cry at the same time. That same month I experienced two more amazing miracles: I was set free from my nicotine addiction and someone paid off all the debt we had accrued on our mortgage. God had done it – and much, much more! He had made the ninety percent stretch further than I imagined possible. Of course, I then needed to humbly apologize to my friend, Chris, who graciously forgave me with a smile on his face. Tithing was my first "raven's food" encounter, but it wouldn't be my last.

Jesus with skin on

Cherith was the place where Elijah would become more than just a prophet who carried God's word. At Cherith he would enter into a new level of covenant relationship with God and would *live the word,* not just preach or declare it. God's people lose their ability to impact nations when they preach one thing and practice another. We are not called simply to declare God's word to nations, we are called to become that word in flesh. I call it *Jesus with skin on.* There is no point, for example, preaching to people that God loves them if we don't *show them* that God loves them. God's Word must become our *lifestyle* not our philosophy. His Word must be who we are, though we know we cannot be a perfect replication of Christ, the complete Word of God in the flesh.

God was breaking Elijah free of all that controlled him so he could deliver Israel from all who controlled her. Elijah was learning to obey God completely, even to his death if necessary. History records that all those God used to greatly impact their generation first had to come to such a place of surrender, willing to give their lives for the sake of His cause. This was Elijah's moment.

Challenged to change

A friend once asked me, "How many Methodists does it take to change a light bulb?" I told him I didn't know. "Change? Change?" came his reply with an appropriately shocked face. (I can make this joke because I have Methodist roots!) I know what he meant. Too many great moves of God have ended up as monuments to what God did in the past. I intend no sleight on the Methodist movement – it can be true of any church or movement. We have a fear of and natural defense against change. We like our comfort zones and stability. Change represents a challenge of faith. It takes faith to leave the comfortable and move forward and many people find this hard.

Even Jesus' disciples struggled with change. When Mary returned to the upper room to inform Peter and the others that Jesus' tomb was open and His body gone, Peter and John immediately ran to see if it was true. Once they had concluded it was indeed true, they left Mary outside the tomb while they returned to the upper room. Mary, brokenhearted and inconsolable, wept at the thought of not being able to see Jesus again. But then He appeared to her, though she didn't recognize Him at first, and asked her why she was weeping. The Bible says,

"She, supposing Him to be the gardener, said to Him, 'Sir, if You have carried Him away, tell me where You have laid Him, and I will take Him away.' Jesus said to her, 'Mary!' She turned and said to Him, 'Rabboni!' (which is to say, Teacher)." (John 20:15-16)

Why didn't Mary recognize Jesus? After all, she had been with Him only three days earlier and had spent the best part of three and a half years on His team. She didn't recognize Him because He had changed! What went into the tomb was not what came out. She only recognized Jesus because He spoke and knew her name! In other words, *Jesus' followers ran past a living Jesus to visit a place He had once been and didn't notice they'd passed Him on the way!*

What a similar problem we have today! Thousands of people will reject attending a church where God's Word is preached thoroughly, week after week, where signs, wonders and miracles happen as freely as in the days of Jesus, in order to attend a church where the Gospel is not clearly preached and there is no evidence of the life and power of God's Spirit. Why would anyone in their right mind want to do this? Because we crave the sense of safety that comes when things remain the same and don't change. It makes us feel we're in control. Change , especially change that takes us by surprise, makes us afraid because we cannot control the situation. We don't like not knowing everything. We don't like not knowing where things will lead. We feel life is out of control when the truth is, we were never in control to begin with – we just liked to think we were!

The disciples were not ready for this change. They found it very difficult to get their heads around the fact that Jesus had been resurrected (I don't blame them) and now they had to grasp that their Lord Jesus had also been transformed.

For the next forty days Jesus met with His followers and repeatedly spoke about the Gospel being taken to the ends of the world. He gave them the amazing revelation that, in fact, the Gospel was not just for the Jews, but also for the Gentiles. The disciples struggled with this seismic shift in their understanding of theology, culture and history. To their minds, God had only ever worked with Israel for thousands of years. Now He was asking them to step outside the box of everything they'd ever known. The cross of Calvary had changed everything.

The disciples struggled for years to cope with this change and it took a major intervention by God into Peter's life (Acts 10:5-28) to help them accept the changes He was bringing to the world. God's power and salvation was not just for Israel, it was for all people. It was only after God's intervention in Cornelius' house that the Apostles purposefully sent out teams to the Gentile nations to preach the Gospel of Jesus Christ (Acts 11:22).

If we do not change and cooperate with what God is saying and doing today, we will begin to die spiritually. He is our life and if He moves on, we must move with Him. He is our provision and if He moves while we remain in the same place through fear of change, His provision for our lives will dry up. This was the lesson the people of God learned quickly in the wilderness. Christianity is not a religion, it is a relationship with God. It is not a set of rules we adhere to or simply "believe" in. His Word is our life, our substance, our health.

"Man shall not live by bread alone but man lives by every word that proceeds from the mouth of the Lord." (Deuteronomy 8:3)

"I am the Bread of life." (John 6:48)

What God plans He provides for

Every day the water in the brook where Elijah drank shrank a little until eventually, just a few drops remained. If Elijah wanted to moisten his lips now, he would have to lie down in order to do it, very aware of the fact that this provision of God was drawing to an end. Here he learned that when God's provision dries up, it is time to move on. He could no longer stay at that place and God's provision must come from another source.

James 5:17-18 says,

"Elijah was a man with a nature like ours, and he prayed earnestly that it would not rain; and it did not rain on the land for three years and six months. And he prayed again, and the heaven gave rain, and the earth produced its fruit."

Circumstances that test us can either cause us to become earnest in our faith or easily persuaded to give up. Some people give up easily at the first sign of a problem, whilst others, who face even greater problems and situations, just grow in faith and determination, refusing to give up. Such people continue to push forward more that ever when a problem arises until eventually they break through. As we've noted previously, we cannot control what happens to us, but we can control what our response will be – the choice is ours.

Elijah's situation deteriorated, but he did not give up. He continued to eagerly pray until he gained his Master's direction. He was to go further into the wilderness and there he would find a widow of Sidon and her son, so impoverished that they were collecting wood to light a fire to cook their final meal before lying down to die. They could no longer brave the effects of the famine and drought on the land (which Elijah had been instrumental in bringing!). But at the point of their deepest despair God sent Elijah to them. *"God works all things together for good"* (Romans 8:28). We read,

"Then the word of the Lord came to him, saying, 'Arise, go to Zarephath, which belongs to Sidon, and dwell there. See, I have commanded a widow there to provide for you.' So he arose and went to Zarephath. And when he came to the gate of the city, indeed a widow was there gathering sticks. And he called to her and said, 'Please bring me a little water in a cup, that I may drink.'

And as she was going to get it, he called to her and said, 'Please bring me a morsel of bread in your hand.'

So she said, 'As the Lord your God lives, I do not have bread, only a handful of flour in a bin, and a little oil in a jar; and see, I am gathering a couple of sticks that I may go in and prepare it for myself and my son, that we may eat it, and die.'

And Elijah said to her, 'Do not fear; go and do as you have said, but make me a small cake from it first, and bring it to me; and afterward make some for yourself and your son. For thus says the Lord God of Israel: "The bin of flour shall not be used up, nor shall the jar of oil run dry, until the day the Lord sends rain on the earth."' So she went away and did according to the word of Elijah; and she and he and her household ate for many days. The bin of flour was not used up, nor did the jar of oil run dry, according to the word of the Lord which He spoke by Elijah." (1 Kings 17:8-16)

God loves the clean and the unclean

The Sidonians were neighbors of Israel. According to the perspective of law-abiding Israelites, therefore, this woman was "unclean"; she was not a "covenant" child of God. But God had taught Elijah to receive from "unclean" ravens, so that in due course he would have no problem receiving from another "unclean" source, the Sidonian widow. God cared so much for this widow and her son that He changed the attitude and perspective of Elijah. Elijah went to her and we see a scriptural principle enacted: the widow offers the first portion of the cake to Elijah (thus offering it to God), and God opens the floodgates of His merciful provision towards her. For the duration of the drought and famine Elijah remained in this widow's home and received Gods provision for his life through this unclean "raven" of Sidon. Like Moses, God had taken Elijah "outside his camp" in order to prepare him, provide for him, and preserve him until His divine timing was fulfilled and the nation of Israel was ready to receive and respond to the word of the Lord.

Frequently, God acts in unthinkable and theologically challenging ways that reveal to us He is not, and cannot, be limited or contained by our understanding, our cultural perspectives and even our theological standpoints. He is so much bigger than our collective attempts at correct theology! God is too concerned with our destiny and His plans to fit neatly into our theological and cultural boxes – most of which are manmade and legalistic in any case. It should not be lost on us that Jesus made mention of this and it offended the Pharisees, the Judaistic preachers of the Law in His day (Luke 4:25).

God loved this Sidonian lady even though she was "unclean" in the eyes of the Law of Israel. Can we not see the connection here? God loves and is concerned for all the people of the world who are "unclean" in the eyes of the Church. He works miracles for the unsaved, despite what Christians think. Today's "unclean" are the unsaved masses, the divorced Christians, those disrespectfully called backsliders, and people who don't adhere to our theological perspectives on life.

A well known preacher recently said that his Sunday services were filled with practicing homosexuals, prostitutes, drug-addicts, the messed up and the broken. He smiled and said, "It's a messy church, just like the one Jesus had 2000 years ago." Many Christians were offended both by the idea of this and his remarks. The feeling behind their offence was this: *you can't let these sorts of people into church to worship God – it's condoning their sinful behavior.* I like to remind people that Jesus never condoned sin or sinful behavior, He just paid for it. He loved the sinner, but not the sin. Sinners flocked around Jesus constantly because He never rejected them. We should be thrilled that we are seeing "these sorts of people" in our meetings. That's why we're here isn't it? The Christians who were offended by this preacher's statement did not understand a simple theological fact: the building we meet in each week is not the church – we are the church. These "unclean" people have not entered "the Church", they have only entered "a building". Only when they repent of their sins and place their faith for salvation in Christ's complete work upon the cross will they have entered into "the Church".

The widow's miracle depended on her doing the most unthinkable thing at that moment. She was to give half of what she had to the man of God who had come to visit, when her own situation was dire. Elijah was asking her to sow in the midst of her greatest famine and trust God to provide for her and her son. The Bible shows that God brought her to that place where she was willing to do whatever was necessary in order to live. And we know that God had completely changed Elijah's perspective by the Brook Cherith. So God had prepared both the miracle worker and the one who needed the miracle. Do you need a miracle? Well, know that God is working to bring you to the place where you're able to receive His directive word – no matter what it is – while at the same time He is arranging the situation or person through which your miracle will come. Don't worry. Just earnestly worship God, trusting He will work it out. Elijah lived with this widow for the remainder of the drought and God's miracle provision continued throughout. God had changed a prophet's nature and perspective and a widow's perspective of life. Now it was time for the nation to choose to change.

People must choose to change

At the end of the drought the Lord spoke to Elijah telling him to find king Ahab and call all of the people of Israel together at Mount Carmel (1 Kings 18:20-40). Three years had passed since the day Elijah first prophesied to Ahab regarding the famine in the land. Ahab had sent his men out to look for Elijah to kill him because the prophecy had come to pass, but they couldn't find him. God had hidden him in an unexpected place, the wilderness of Zarephath, Sidon. No one expected Elijah to be found among the Sidonians any more than they expected Moses to be among the Midianites! God sometimes hides us away, not to hurt us, but to keep us from harm until it is His timing to reveal us.

Now it was God's timing to turn His people back to Him and He had faithfully prepared a man to open the windows of Heaven as never before, turning every heart back to the Lord in one superb moment. Whilst preparing a *man* for the *moment* to deliver His *message*, God had used three years of famine and drought to bring His people to a place where they were willing to change! What a painful process to go through to accept God's will.

Must individuals, churches or denominations be brought to the brink of spiritual or physical death or catastrophe before they are willing to listen to God's word – even if it means great change is necessary? If the way we are doing life, church or ministry is not working, then something needs to change. This is obvious. Doing the same thing over and over for years, expecting a different outcome, is madness. Church life today stands at the crossroads of opportunity. We stand on the brink of the greatest revival mankind has ever known, but to receive it we must allow God to tear up our old wineskins. Church as we know it is coming to an end and will soon be no more. The church experience we are being offered is like nothing we've ever known. It is all about people, not politics, about building families and societies more than monumental buildings. It will be about His kingdom, not ours. It will be about meeting with Him, not meetings to fulfill man's agendas. It will be all about a leadership serving a multitude of people to release their gifts and ministries to fulfill His vision, not about thousands of Christians going inside a building three or four times a week to fulfill the vision and ministry of the man on the platform. It will be an upside down, inside out Church!

We have church life completely the wrong way around. We are consumed with going into a building called "church" instead of going as His Church out into the world! We are more concerned with the heating in our buildings than the fire in our hearts, the comfort of our bodies more than our soul being discomforted by the torment of millions of lost people going to Hell. We spend millions of dollars or pounds and man hours on buildings, lighting, air-conditioning, sound equipment, media presentations, literature, Bible classes and much, much more, yet we are more ineffective now in taking the Gospel to our cities than at any time in the past. We are passionate about our buildings, but not so passionate about Him in our hearts!

Church leaders use manipulative and controlling methods to keep their people attending services each week and become fearful when someone visits another church in the city. I'm sure some people reading this will be annoyed by my comments, but I don't mean to offend anyone. This is the cry of a man of God with over thirty years experience of church leadership and ministry, who has a burden to see God's will implemented in our lives. I want to protect us from the pain we will experience if we don't hear the word of the Lord and change.

Let me assure you, the Church of the future will be one Church across a region with a leadership that oversees not controls. The people will be *gathered together* for worship, not segregated across the city. It will be based more in cell groups and homes than church buildings. "The Church" will meet in offices, factories, schools and a multitude of diverse places. They will meet because of locality not denomination, stream or style. Christians will meet in their neighborhoods to pray, worship and evangelize together in their communities, because that is the biblical pattern. The Church needs to come back into alignment with God's blueprint!

Both Moses and Elijah had been prepared by God for their mission through painful and seemingly strange events. Both had their hearts and nature changed. The men who went out into the desert were not the men who came back after God had finished His work in them. Both were changed by incredibly challenging, painful situations. But both became men God used to bring His people out of bondage and slavery to false gods. Both were prophets and both opened the windows of Heaven in their generation (Exodus 19:19; 24:8; 33:10; 40:34; 1 Kings 18:38). This is why they were qualified to stand beside Jesus on the Mount of Transfiguration that day. They knew what Jesus was being asked to do. He was being asked to bring the ultimate change to life. The cross was looming ahead and Gethsemane was going to be His greatest struggle as He accepted God's will and word above His own desires. It would be in Gethsemane that Jesus would swap wills and lives with God to fulfill His purpose. It would be on Calvary that He would open the windows of Heaven permanently for the first time since Adam. Adam's sin had closed the door of Heaven (Genesis 3:24), but the death and resurrection of Jesus would open the way for all sin to be paid for, swept away and for all mankind to receive forgiveness and salvation – to be changed from darkness to light. The way to God would be opened once again.

CHAPTER 8

LOST!

The parables of the lost sheep, the lost coin and the prodigal son found in Luke 15 all show that the Lord is a God of grace and that His grace is lavishly outrageous. God's grace seems foolish in the eyes of the world because it doesn't appear logical. Let's take a closer look at the impact God's grace has on us and how we can extend it to others.

The lost sheep

What shepherd in his right mind leaves ninety-nine sheep that are safe to go and search for one that is lost? Surely the ninety-nine sheep will have scattered by the time he returns with the missing one? Sheep don't need any encouragement to wander, they do it instinctively! That's why shepherds put them in pens, to prevent them straying and placing themselves in danger. No wonder God calls us His sheep (Psalm 100:3)!

But reading this parable over and over doesn't reveal any deeper message Jesus is trying to communicate. It is *foolish!* It doesn't make any sense, but it illustrates God's grace. The ninety-nine sheep could have grounds for complaint: "It's not *fair* to leave us to search for the lost one. We've been obedient; he hasn't!" And of course, they'd be right. Grace isn't reasonable. It's not *fair*. If you want what is reasonable and *fair* then go to Hell! Hell is what would be *fair* for us. Aren't you glad God is not *fair?*

The lost coin

In this parable we hear about a woman who has lost a coin and turns her house upside down, searching relentlessly to find it. Jesus says that the woman's earnest attitude reflects the attitude and motivation of Father God. He tells us that Heaven rejoices when one sinner repents, (i.e. the lost coin is found and returned to its rightful owner).

When Adam sinned it was driven by his own flawed motivation. God, who is holy, pure and perfect, had done nothing to provoke or cause Adam to stumble. In fact, He had given his son perfect fathering and a perfect life. It was Adam who rejected God's ways through his blindness. Despite this, God's attitude was not, "Let him find his own way back then" or "He deserves everything he's going to get." Rather, the Father's immediate response was to go looking for Adam. God looked for Adam and Eve until He found them and then set about paying the price for their sin Himself. God never asked Adam to pay the price for the mess he'd caused, He went straight out and put into action His plan to cover the cost, not just of Adam's sin, but the whole of mankind's. This is nothing less than lavish, undeserved grace – and Heaven explodes in jubilation when one more person accepts this grace and the free gift of salvation.

Is this not totally unheard of, abnormal, unreasonable, illogical and unfair? Yes, it is all this and more because that's what grace is like. God's forgiveness, reconciliation and redemption are illogical and unfair. But it is this grace which caused Jesus to leave Heaven and come to earth to take on human flesh; this grace which kept Him on the cross until His work of redemption was complete – thus ensuring that people who trust in Him don't have to go to hell, even though they cannot be perfect. That is *pure grace.* God punished Christ upon the cross so that you and I don't need to receive the punishment for our sin. What an incredible loving Father God is. All we need do is to recognize we are sinners needing a Savior, because we cannot live a perfect enough life to gain entrance to Heaven, and then receive His forgiveness for our sinfulness.

The lost son

The third parable Jesus tells in Luke 15 is that of the prodigal son. Notice again that the father in the illustration is just not reasonable in his actions! He does not act like any natural father would. He gives his son half of all he has, knowing full well what will happen, and then watches as his son turns away and distances himself from his father. The wealth didn't corrupt the boy, it just exposed issues that had been there all along, hidden deep within and never addressed. This son had unfinished business with his father that needed to be dealt with. The father's actions provided a way to bring the issue to the surface, for it to be addressed and dealt with once and for all.

Although we are not told why this son harbored unforgiveness or resentment towards his father (the root of all his problems), we see the evidence or fruit of the problem manifest itself in the way he conducts his life. The son withdrew from the father and went his own way. His un-dealt with issues caused him to look elsewhere for what he thought he needed to fulfill his life. He went looking for whatever it was he felt he wasn't getting from his father.

Guard your heart

If there is one thing we need to discover here it is the truth that our heart governs our life.

"Keep your heart with all diligence, for out of it spring the issues of life." (Proverbs 4:23)

What we believe in our heart about ourselves, or anyone else, governs everything we do and become. It influences the way we dress, the way we live, the friends we keep, the way we think, talk and walk. It orders our actions and reactions.

In the prodigal son we see a young man's "heart issues" explode into the open for all to see. They destroy everything good in his life until all he can see are the "negatives" (as he perceives them) about his father and his life. His heart sets in motion a series of events that lead him into the "pig swill" of life. Things could scarcely get worse. But at this point he becomes ready to deal with the *real* problem. Eventually, the things we run from catch up with us and our loving heavenly Father provides us with the grace and the opportunity to deal with our pain.

Where was father while his lost son was learning these tough lessons? As close to his son as he could get. Day after day he looked for his son and waited at the edge of his kingdom. He knew the boy must return one day. When that day arrived you can imagine the father jumping up and down, shouting to his servants that his lost son is on the horizon and coming home. Many people I have met have never seen a father like this. They experienced a disciplinarian or a distant, cold father. Others tell me they had good fathers who loved them, but who never jumped up and down in ecstasy over them. Sadly our earthly fathers have been conditioned to be like that. But our heavenly Father is not that way. Zephaniah 3:17 tells us that,

"The Lord your God in your midst, the Mighty One, will save; he will rejoice over you with gladness, he will quiet you with His love, he will rejoice over you with singing."

This incredible scripture says that God the Father rejoices and sings over us! To "rejoice" here means to be exceedingly happy, to celebrate. It can also mean to leap up and down and spin round like a spinning top. The Hebrew word used here for "singing" means to "shout", "proclaim from a place of joy" or to give a "victorious shout". The picture is clear: God is crazy about us. He leaps about in exuberant joy, shouting as loud as He can over YOU! Do you visualize Him like this when you come into His presence? If not, why not? Is it because you feel insignificant?

One day I returned home, having been away on a ministry trip for several days, and parked my car on the driveway. I had barely stepped out of the car when my front door burst open and, with great energy, my little daughter came running towards me as fast as she could, holding out her arms to be hugged. She leapt full tilt towards me, actually forcing me to drop everything I had in my hands so that I could catch her! The momentum of her leap made me not only catch her, but swing her around in circles. As I did, I kissed her over and over saying, "I love you!" This is the scene described by Zephaniah. The Father is doing the very same thing to us! I thought about that very scripture as I held my daughter and was overwhelmed to the point of tears to think my heavenly Father could possibly feel or react in such a way every time I come into His presence. It healed me. It is still healing me. It gave me a confidence I never had before – the confidence to dare to believe He really does love me unconditionally and lavishly.

As the prodigal son drew close to home he must have been able to see his father standing, waiting. I'm sure his heart was pounding at the prospect of having to acknowledge his gross foolishness and sin. When they finally came together, the son began reciting a speech of repentance he'd been rehearsing over and over, but the father stopped him in his tracks and silenced the speech. There was no need for him to say anything; no need for his son to grovel and re-earn respect or favor; no need for his son to weep and wail and experience his father's disapproval. Not once do we hear his father saying, "You foolish boy, I told you so!" His father didn't force him live through an awkward atmosphere of displeasure, experiencing his simmering anger. He didn't tell him it would be a long time before he could be trusted again. He didn't tell him he was reluctant to take him back, but had begrudgingly come around to the idea. None of this. The father immediately restored his son to his rightful place. Once a son, always a son!

I know – it doesn't make sense! It is illogical and unfair – just ask the boy's older brother. It's called *grace* – undeserved, unearned and lavish.

The reaction of other people to God's grace in our lives is fascinating. Look at the anger and frustration that quickly bubbles to the surface of the father's eldest son. He was absolutely livid. Notice that the father now offers him an opportunity to deal with *his* unresolved heart issues – of which there are clearly a few. Sadly, we don't see him respond well. He doesn't experience the wonder of grace for himself in healing and reconciliation. Instead he keeps the battle raging. But that's a story for a different message!

A truth to set you free

Reflect for a moment on all that God does for us in His mercy:

- The Gospel of Jesus Christ is the Gospel of *grace*. Grace is God doing for us what we can't do for ourselves.

- There is a price to pay for our sin, so before we were even born He paid it for us through the death of His Son (Romans 3:23-24; Romans 5:8; Ephesians 1:4)

- We cannot change our heart – it is always self-centered – so He gives us a new one (Ezekiel 36:26)

- We cannot stop our sin and be perfect, so He makes us

perfectly acceptable in His eyes through the blood of
Jesus, His Son (Ephesians 1:6)

- Then He gives us the same spirit as His Son, Jesus Christ
  (Romans 8:11)

Mercy is not getting what we deserve, while grace is getting what
we don't. As God grants us His mercy and grace in our life, so we
are faced with a choice: either we choose to live by mercy and
grace ourselves or, by default, we choose legalism and judgment.
Much of what people call "religion" is nothing more than legalism
and judgmentalism that stems from a guilty awareness of our sin.
All we need to do is accept that *"all fall short of the glory of God"*
(Romans 3:23) and therefore need a Savior. Instead, people
commit themselves to the ridiculous straightjacket of external
performance, trying to be perfect to meet the required standard of
holiness.

When we fail to live in grace and mercy we end up expecting
those around us to be perfect and become angry and judgmental
when they fail. In turn, their failure to meet our expectations
backfires on us, making us realize that neither do we live perfectly.
But instead of accepting that it is impossible to live a perfect life
(which is why we need a Savior), we lash out, highlighting
people's faults, weaknesses and flaws. So many people live like
this because they have not accepted and appropriated God's lavish
grace. They may have committed their lives to Christ, but still be
entrenched in their own guilt. God's grace must be allowed to
pierce the hardness of our proud hearts so that we can emerge
from behind our masks of pretence and stand "naked" before God
as Adam did, but without shame.

We so easily forget that the blood of Jesus did not *cover* our sin,
but completely *removed* it from us – and not just our past sins, but
all our sin. Jesus died not only for the *sins* we commit (the fruit),

but for the *sin* we were born into (the root), passed onto us by Adam. We don't have to feel forever guilty for our *sins* because He has destroyed the power of sin and death and removed the root of guilt. Instead Jesus has given us His righteousness.

In the Old Testament sacrifices were continually offered for the sins of Israel. Once a year, on the Day of Atonement, the High Priest would make the required sacrifices and go through the temple, beyond the veil, into the Most Holy Place. He would worship the Lord, confess the sins of Israel, and pour out the blood of the sacrifices onto the Mercy Seat which rested on the Ark of the Covenant. If the sacrifices had been carried out correctly then God would speak to the High Priest telling him that Israel's sins were "appeased" or "covered over" for one more year. The New Testament tells us that, prophetically, all this pointed to Christ. But the difference is, the offering of His perfect life and death upon the cross was not a sacrifice to *cover over* sin, but rather to completely *obliterate* it. The Old Covenant way of receiving forgiveness was through the shed blood of sacrifices; the New Covenant way is by faith in the Lamb of God who, *"takes away the sin of the world"* (John 1:29)

The Bible tells us that Christ's sacrifice destroyed sin's power so thoroughly and removed sin so far from those who trust in Him that God remembers it no more Hebrews 8:12). I ask the question: if God chooses not to remember our sin any more, why do we keep reminding ourselves of it all the time? This is "Old Covenant" thinking. The Old Testament sacrifices reminded the people that they could not live perfectly and kept them conscious of their failure to live up to the demands of the Law.

"In those sacrifices there is a reminder of sins every year. For it is not possible that the blood of bulls and goats could take away sins." (Hebrews 10:3-4)

The New Testament is all about learning to forgive ourselves and forget our failures and be ever so thankful to God for His forgiveness and the fact that He imputes to us (gives to us) His own righteousness. The writer to the Hebrews stated that the Old Covenant was obsolete, out of date and ready to vanish. Christ has established a New Covenant, superior in every way (Hebrews 8:12-13). Why is it then, that so little of our preaching is set towards helping Christians understand that He has made us perfectly righteous through Christ – that God no longer has a "sin problem" because He dealt with it at the cross? Rather than constantly preaching repentance, keeping the body of Christ sin-conscious, we should be preaching the message of God's grace. If we are truly born again we are no longer sinners, but saints (Acts 9:32). We don't need to focus on our failure but on His work of perfection. I am not saying a Christian never sins. There are times when we have to acknowledge our sin and put it right with God and others. But we need not make our imperfection and flaws our constant focus. Instead we need to encourage one another to grow in faith in His grace and mercy.

"But now the righteousness of God apart from the law is revealed, being witnessed by the Law and the Prophets, even the righteousness of God, through faith in Jesus Christ, to all and on all who believe. For there is no difference; for all have sinned and fall short of the glory of God, being justified freely by His grace through the redemption that is in Christ Jesus, whom God set forth as a propitiation by His blood, through faith, to demonstrate His righteousness, because in His forbearance God had passed over the sins that were previously committed, to demonstrate at the present time His righteousness, that He might be just and the justifier of the one who has faith in Jesus. Where is boasting then? It is excluded. By what law? Of works? No, but by the law of faith. Therefore we conclude that a man is justified by faith apart from the deeds of the law." (Romans 3:20-28)

Old Testament or New Testament believers?

I want to ask you a challenging question: which covenant are you living in today – the Old or the New? Are you living under grace free from guilt and condemnation, or do you find yourself succumbing to a performance-based lifestyle you can never live up to?

The Old Covenant, also called the "Law and the Prophets" (Matthew 7:12) has been superceded and along with it, guilt, shame and the constant reminder of sin have been taken away. Throughout the New Testament the message of Christ is never referred to as the "Law and the Prophets". Instead it is the "Gospel of the kingdom" (Matthew 4:23) the "Gospel of Jesus Christ" (Mark 1:1), the "Gospel of Grace" (Acts 20:24), the "Gospel of God" (Romans 1:1), the "Gospel of His Son" (Romans 1:9), the "Gospel of Christ" (Romans 1:16), the "Gospel of Peace" (Romans 10:15) and the "Gospel of our Lord Jesus Christ" (2 Thessalonians 1:8). Can you see the liberating power of Jesus? Through Him we have been brought into an altogether new dimension of living.

The New Testament shows over and over again that we are to stay in the place of faith and believe that what Christ did upon the cross was enough for us to be acceptable to God. We do not need to add anything to what He has done for us – it is enough. We strive to keep an attitude of faith in Him, but we do not strive to live up to a set of religious rules, because we are no longer *lost!*

CHAPTER 9

I ONCE WAS BLIND, BUT NOW I SEE

"What is it?" I enquired standing in my friend Kev's living room. I was pondering a piece of his own artwork hanging on the fireplace wall. I tilted my head one way, then the other trying to figure it out. To me it just looked like random squiggles, abstract lines and an obscure image in pencil. "What do you think it is?" came his annoying reply. I wanted to respond, "If I knew that I wouldn't be asking, would I?" For some reason his answer really irritated me – I didn't know why. Perhaps it was because I felt foolish and a bit frustrated. After all, shouldn't the subject matter of a picture be obvious? "This isn't art as it should be," I thought to myself. Surely Kev intended his picture to reveal something to me, but I just couldn't see it and that bugged me.

Kev brought me a long awaited coffee and stood there smiling. I questioned him but he refused to explain his picture to me! He was happy because his artwork was doing exactly what he wanted it to do. "When I drew it," he told me, "I did it in such a way that people couldn't just look at it and know immediately what I wanted to communicate. I want people to look at it and ponder, then ponder some more and learn to see with a new perspective."

Now he had lost me. Was there more than one way to "see" it? I mean, if you want to draw a picture of a mountain, for instance, then why not make it look like a mountain! Why make it difficult? I laughed and told him I thought modern art was a lot of bizarre nonsense. He was patient with me and said no, in fact, what was happening to me was what he intended. The picture was demanding of me that I change my perspective and use a different way of seeing. He actually wanted to induce in the observer the frustration of not knowing what it was! Even to the point of irritation, so that they would revisit the image again and again until they could "see" the message.

I had to agree with his theory. Had the drawing been "obvious" I probably would have studied it for a few seconds, said "That's nice" and then moved on. But Kev had managed to engage my attention and stir my emotions. Now I was examining it repeatedly with great curiosity, compelled to discover its hidden message. Throughout my visit Kev sat there and chuckled at me, because in the midst of chatting to him my eyes would stray back to the picture, hoping the message would jump out at me so I could tell him, "I've got it!" But it didn't.

Just then the phone rang and Kev left the room, giving me the chance to stare at the picture and absorb it, rather than getting frustrated with it. I was distracted by the sound of a car outside and I looked out the window for a couple of minutes. Then I turned to look at the picture again and there it was! It was as though I had suffered from temporary blindness, because in front of me was an image of the cross of Calvary and Jesus reaching out to me from it. I had finally decoded the image. It was so powerful that instead of happily shouting, "Aha, I've got it!" I stood silently, drinking in the immense compassion it communicated. It was so arresting that a tear escaped from my eye and trickled down my cheek. I was ambushed unexpectedly by the inexplicable, overwhelming goodness and kindness of God towards me.

Kev returned to the room. He saw me and knew I'd understood. He put his arm around my shoulder and thanked Jesus out loud for helping me to "see" the hidden message of the cross. I had been impacted in a fresh way. The cross had been right in front of me all the time, yet it was hidden. All it took for me to see it was to look from a new perspective. When I "saw" it, a moment of sheer grace had taken place as God revealed to me the unfathomable riches of His kingdom. His character and nature were there for all to see, but "hidden", like a father hides Christmas presents – not because He doesn't want his kids to have them, but so that they will know the joy of discovering them at the appropriate moment.

Repeatedly, God has worked like this in my life and ministry. We can read over and over again the truths written in His Word, but there are certain things we simply don't "see" until one of these magical grace moments occurs and suddenly, something fresh is revealed.

Below is one particular verse of scripture that I had read numerous times and had meant very little to me. But one day God took this verse, brought it to life, and deeply impacted me, just like Kev's drawing had done. Read it with me right now and see what happens to you.

"And when they heard that He was alive and had been seen by her, they did not believe. After that, He appeared in another form to two of them as they walked and went into the country. And they went and told it to the rest, but they did not believe them either." (Mark 16:11-13)

Did you see something? Read it again. Can you see something utterly astounding? There is something hidden here that is probably never preached by the majority of churches in the world. I have never heard anyone else preach on this nor read a book that covered the issue. Don't worry if you can't "see" it yet – that's the whole point! I want this scripture to bug you as it did me! I want you to read it and see five words that don't make sense to the natural mind. If you have already seen it, you are probably trying to grasp the meaning of it. Can it possibly be saying what we think it is saying and, if so, what can it mean? Hopefully, by the end of this book you'll be in awe, as I was, of its hidden message.

But first let me set the scene and unpack the background to this event by guiding you through a four-day journey that Jesus took His disciples on before this miracle on the Emmaus Road.

CHAPTER 10

DON'T KICK THE DONKEY, RIDE IT!

"Now when they drew near Jerusalem, to Bethphage and Bethany, at the Mount of Olives, He sent two of His disciples; and He said to them, 'Go into the village opposite you; and as soon as you have entered it you will find a colt tied, on which no one has sat. Loose it and bring it. And if anyone says to you, "Why are you doing this?" say, "The Lord has need of it," and immediately he will send it here.'

So they went their way, and found the colt tied by the door outside on the street, and they loosed it. But some of those who stood there said to them, 'What are you doing, loosing the colt?'

And they spoke to them just as Jesus had commanded. So they let them go. Then they brought the colt to Jesus and threw their clothes on it, and He sat on it. And many spread their clothes on the road, and others cut down leafy branches from the trees and spread them on the road." (Mark 11:1-8)

"Now in the morning, as they passed by, they saw the fig tree dried up from the roots. And Peter, remembering, said to Him, 'Rabbi, look! The fig tree which You cursed has withered away.' So Jesus answered and said to them, 'Have faith in God. For assuredly, I say to you, whoever says to this mountain, "Be removed and be cast into the sea," and does not doubt in his heart, but believes that those things he says will come to pass, he will have whatever he says.'" (Mark 11 :20-23)

When Jesus made the statement above, it was during the final week of His earthly life and ministry. If, like Jesus, we knew we were living through our last few days on earth, would we not want to say the most important things we could think of? Would we not take time to give our final instructions, words of encouragement, advice or affirmation to those we loved? We would certainly not waste our time as we spent our last precious hours.

During the final days of His earthly life Jesus spent three of them marching His disciples back and forth from Bethany to Jerusalem. We must understand as we read this account that Jesus *knew* He was living His last days, but His disciples didn't. At this point they still assumed He would be around for many years to come. They didn't anticipate that anything major was about to change in their lives. But the truth was, everything they thought was unchangeable and stable was about to be blown apart. They were about to enter the greatest season of transition they had ever personally known, as Jesus took them closer and closer to a date with divine destiny.

The disciples don't know yet that they are about to enter a period of grief, turmoil and confusion, so their reactions and attitudes are no different than at other times in their life with Jesus. Because Jesus *knows* these are His last days with them, He is purposefully trying to prepare them for their transition from being followers to leaders; from being those who watched and heard Him minister, to those who could do it without Him. He is preparing them for His death and their entry into an arena vastly different from anything they have imagined or prepared for. Notice how Jesus helps them through this process.

They arrive outside the villages of Bethany and Bethphage on the Mount of Olives. Bethany is where Lazarus, Mary and Martha live. Jesus has stayed here many times before and will do so for the next few days. But He does not go immediately into Bethany. He stays outside and tells the disciples to enter the village where they will find a colt outside on the street, tied to the door of a house. Most people have heard sermons on Jesus asking for the colt to fulfill this scripture:

"Rejoice greatly, O daughter of Zion! Shout, O daughter of Jerusalem! Behold, your King is coming to you; he is just and having salvation, lowly and riding on a donkey, a colt, the foal of a donkey." (Zechariah 9:9)

Zechariah prophesied that Jesus would enter Jerusalem riding on a donkey and Jesus did indeed fulfill this scripture with His actions. But fulfilling the scripture does not tell us *why* Jesus did this at this time. There was more to the life of Jesus than just fulfilling a selection of scriptures.

New mentors for new experiences

When you were a small child of about six years old, you went to school and learned under the tuition of trained teachers. But when you matured and entered senior education you came under the oversight of new teachers who were equipped for that level of tutoring. The same principle applied when you left your local school and went to college or university. Each level of growth, maturity and development has to be accompanied by new tutors. So it is in our spiritual lives.

Could it be that Jesus was showing us that when a time of transition is upon us He will already have placed what we need close to hand – a "mentor" to help us move from our "Bethany" to our "Jerusalem", from glory to glory, from one level to the next? For us to fulfill the dreams and desires of our heart and God's destiny for our lives, we must accept that changes and transitions have to happen in our lives. If we don't accept this we will remain where we are and stay the way we are. If we want to experience a different dimension of living then we must rise to a new level of understanding, insight and belief.

Because we can easily get stuck in our beliefs, and our beliefs are what order our actions, we frequently need someone or something to change our perceptions and alter our belief system. When this happens we are able to make the necessary transition from where we are to where we are supposed to be.

In His infinite mercy, the Lord provides us with what we need (whether it looks like a blessing or not) for every stage of our life. He provides something to help us negotiate our transitions. It is this I have called my "donkey." But donkeys can kick and bite as well as carry people and are sometimes stubborn and won't move when we tell them to. The circumstances of life can be just the same. God's way of moving us towards His destiny for our lives is not always through seasons of blessing! Sometimes strange, unexpected and even painful events impact our lives and disturb our sense of "peace". But within these events He is present and will enable us to overcome the trial or test. The event that looked like it had come to destroy us actually has the ability to help us transition to a new level of knowledge, experience, authority or whatever God knows we need at that time.

The donkey Jesus wanted was tied up at a door out on the street. Doors are places of transition – they enable us to leave one arena and enter another. Spiritually speaking, a door represents a place where we let go of all we've known to receive all we've desired or dreamed of, but never experienced. It is a place of "closing off" all that is familiar to step into the unknown and embrace the unfamiliar. Frequently God asks us to "let go" of something in order to "lay hold" of something else, and a "donkey" is waiting somewhere close by to help you do it!

Change is always resisted

We will always encounter resistance whenever we seriously make up our minds to make changes in our lives that will cause us to grow in Christ and glorify His name. Satan knows that when we are changed to become more Christlike we will carry more of His authority, more of His power and grace. It is the anointing of God that destroys the bondage of Satan's lies in our life, so our enemy will not want us to change.

Notice how we have an immense craving for food right after we have decided to fast for the day! Notice how, when the Holy Spirit tells us to do something, we begin to struggle with doubt as a voice asks us, "Are you sure it was God who spoke to you?" It was the same for the disciples. Just as they put their hands on the reins of the donkey they encountered a challenge to their obedience: *"What are you doing loosing the colt?"* (v5) came the voice of resistance.

I remember when I first heard the call of God on my life to preach His Gospel. The Holy Spirit clearly showed me that if I obeyed and answered His call, He would take me to the furthest corners of the world, put me on platforms that would cause my voice to be heard by millions of people, and I would see multitudes saved and healed by His power. Instantly, the voice of doubt and resistance began to shout loud and clear: "Who do you think you are that God would use you so powerfully after all the things you've done wrong in your life?" It wasn't really a question, but an accusation about my past. I was immediately forced to make a choice. I could listen to the voice of accusation and "reason" and therefore never believe my life could be worthwhile or significant, or I could listen to the voice of faith calling me to believe in the blood of Christ, His forgiveness, and trust Him implicitly. One voice condemned me. One voice inspired and gave me a hope of a better way of life. I chose the voice of the Holy Spirit.

I had many hurdles and mountains of doubt to overcome in the years that followed my decision to believe in His call, but I can boldly say to you now that He has accomplished His promise to me and done above and beyond what I ever thought was possible for a young man who grew up in the mining valleys of Wales. He *has* taken me around the world many times and He has caused me to be in places where I could preach to millions of people and see many people healed and find Christ as their personal Savior. He did it just as He said He would.

They spoke just as Jesus did

When the disciples were challenged they had a choice to make. To cower down under the voice of opposition that wanted to crush their faith and obedience, or to rise up and speak against it.

By the time we have finished studying this portion of Mark 11, you will have noticed that one of the central things Jesus teaches His disciples in these last hours of His life is the power of the spoken word.

People said of Jesus that,

"They were astonished at His teaching, for His word was with authority." (Luke 4:32)

When Jesus spoke His voice was filled with authority. Not volume, just authority. A well respected evangelist friend once said to me that authority is like a bar of soap – the more you have to use it, the less you have! But when you have genuine God-given authority you just speak and things begin to happen.

(As an aside, it is an interesting study to look up the word "authority" in the four gospels in Strong's Concordance and see how often Jesus' authority was challenged).

The authority of Jesus was being challenged as the two disciples loosed the donkey. They were obeying Jesus so it was, in fact, a direct challenge to *His* authority in their lives. It says in verse 6 that they,

"Spoke to them just as Jesus ..."

The disciples spoke with authority to the voice of opposition. They realized this voice of intimidation, fear, guilt and accusation was trying to prevent them breaking through to a new level of the power of God in their lives. We must do the same if we desire to become all He says we can become.

Bethany, Bethphage and Jerusalem

Bethany means "house of poverty" or "house of lack". Bethphage means "house of unripe figs". Poverty and lack is easily understood, but what is the "house of unripe figs" communicating to us?

If a fruit has not ripened we know that something must have stopped its natural development to maturity. An unripe fruit is an "immature" fruit. Another word for immature is "childish". Unripe fruit can also be hard and bitter because of its underdevelopment. Bethphage then, represents a place in life where many are stuck. They live in immaturity and childishness because something has halted their development. They may also have become hardened and bitter through this underdevelopment.

In life, many things happen to us that we don't plan for. Often we are impacted by the words or actions of others. Have you ever been offended or hurt by someone? Of course you have. Life is one long study of the art of forgiveness! If you live in a family, belong to a church, work with other people or just drive a car you'll know exactly what I mean.

Offences against us are inevitable. Jesus said, *"Offences must come"* (Matthew 18:7). As we have said, we cannot control what events happen to us, only the way in which we respond to them. When someone offends us, if we don't respond in a godly way forgiving the offender, then the offence will enter our mind and emotions and linger there. If we don't deal with it and evict it from our soul, eventually it will become lodged in our heart. When this happens we develop an "issue" that begins to affect what we believe, which in turn affects our perceptions, the way we speak and the way we live. Unresolved issues inhibit our growth and shrivel up our ability to be fruitful. They transport us to an unwelcome stay in "Bethpage".

I have known many Christians who became "saved, satisfied and stuck" in their walk with God due to harboring offence instead of releasing forgiveness. We need to see the bigger picture and remember that,

"We do not wrestle against flesh and blood, but against principalities, against powers, against the rulers of the darkness of this age, against spiritual hosts of wickedness in the heavenly places. Therefore take up the whole armor of God, that you may be able to withstand in the evil day, and having done all, to stand." (Ephesians 6:12-13)

Ultimately our problem is not with those who offend us but with the spirit of offence and accusation that is attacking us through life's circumstances. Jesus said that,

"The thief does not come except to steal, and to kill, and to destroy. I have come that they may have life, and that they may have it more abundantly." (John 10:10)

We are fighting a spiritual battle and the demonic strategies launched against us to prevent us from believing what God says. The enemy wants to gain access to our hearts and influence us negatively so that we believe a lie. This is what he did with Adam and Eve in the beginning and he still employs this simple tactic today. Using our shield of faith and making sure we release forgiveness to those who have hurt us prevents demonic power from gaining its desired hold on us.

Returned to completeness

In our examination of Bethany, Bethpage and Jerusalem we see that the latter means "Foundations of Peace." Foundations are what we lay before we erect a building to give strength and stability to the structure. A foundation is something solid, immovable, unshakeable and dependable. The "peace" part of this word means more than simply the absence of conflict or turmoil; it is the word shalom which means "to make good or perfect again", "to make prosper" and to "restore, recompense, complete and make safe in body, mind and estate".

Encapsulated in Jerusalem, then, was the complete opposite of both Bethany and Bethpage – even though they were geographically close to one another. Just seven miles and a hill was all that separated Jerusalem from those other places. What does this tell us? We are always closer to our breakthrough than we think! Often it is only "steps" away and the Lord has provided what we need to carry us from our "house of poverty" to our place of peace, prosperity, completeness and restoration. We must learn not to kick our donkey, but ride it!

Some Bible teachers have suggested that all good things come from God, whilst bad things come from the devil. This superficial and simplistic view causes people to embrace everything that seems good to them and fight against everything they perceive as being negative. Underlying this view is the belief that God would never allow negative things to come into our life because they are bad and He is good! But any loving, responsible parent will tell you that you sometimes have to allow things to come into our children's lives that they perceive as "bad" when it is for their own good! Kids frequently reject green vegetables and salad and want pizza or burgers, but a good parent will insist on and impose what the child perceives as "bad" for the sake of their health. Often stuff looks bad to children that is actually good for them!

There are times in the gym when I am halfway through an hour-long program of exercise, that my body screams at me to stop doing this harmful thing, be sensible and go find a sauna, a sun-bed or a coffee lounge and take it easy! Yet the pain and discipline I endure is what's good for me, not the coffee lounge.

Everything that looks "good" is not always good for us and things we perceive as "bad" God can use for our good. The Bible is full of examples. Often what looked like a devastating blow for God's people turned out to be God's way of giving them the breakthrough they were crying out for.

Delivered from Egypt

One such occasion is when Moses, sent of the Lord, confronts Pharaoh and demands the release of God's people from slavery. When Moses first appeared to the elders of Israel, they believed he was God's answer to their prayers for deliverance. But only one day into the process they change their minds and are angry with him. Why? Because the situation looked like it was taking a turn for the worse. Pharaoh was so annoyed at Moses' insistence that Israel should be set free, that he punished the slaves with a heavier workload. It looked like their donkey was kicking them. Ten times God honored Moses by sending plagues onto the land of Egypt as a punishment on Pharaoh, but Israel had to endure turmoil as this process was unfolding. Moses persevered in faith and eventually millions of people were led out of bondage into new found freedom and prosperity. The pain they endured was necessary for their good and for destiny to be fulfilled.

The Red Sea crossing

The people of God were fleeing Egypt and had arrived at the Red Sea. How was Moses going to lead the people across this great expanse of water which stood between them and their freedom? While every eye looked to Moses for a solution, the message came from the scouts at the rear of the camp that Pharaoh had amassed his army and was heading full speed towards them. With a seemingly immovable sea to the front and a mad Pharaoh to their rear, their death and destruction seemed inevitable. They let Moses know their feelings in no uncertain terms:

"Then they said to Moses, 'Because there were no graves in Egypt, have you taken us away to die in the wilderness? Why have you so dealt with us, to bring us up out of Egypt? Is this not the word that we told you in Egypt, saying, "Let us alone that we may serve the Egyptians?" For it would have been better for us to serve the Egyptians than that we should die in the wilderness.'"

Regardless of the good things the Lord had done for them, they could only see the negative. Fear and unbelief took over their hearts and out of their mouths came anger and bitterness. They believed God had used Moses to bring the plagues and miracles to set them free from Pharaoh for one purpose only: to punish them with a wicked end! Angrily they cried out that it would have been easier and safer to have stayed as slaves. WOW! Their slavery was not made from chains, taskmasters or a nation called Egypt; their slavery was their internal belief system. They had forgotten already that when Moses had first returned to Egypt with the news that God had sent him to bring deliverance, they were delighted and thankful:

"Then Moses and Aaron went and gathered together all the elders of the children of Israel. And Aaron spoke all the words which the Lord had spoken to Moses. Then he did the signs in the sight of

*the people. So the people **believed**; and when they heard that the Lord had visited the children of Israel and that He had looked on their affliction, then they bowed their heads and **worshipped.**"* (Exodus 4:29-31)

They believed, trusted and were firmly convinced that God had sent Moses to set them free from Pharaoh. They were so thankful that they fell down on their faces and honored God. Yet, here they are right on the verge of their deliverance from slavery, about to step into the blessing of God's abundant provision for their lives, and accusations towards Moses tumble out of their hearts and mouths.

They had forgotten their thankfulness to God for Moses. They had forgotten the miracles God had performed to secure their freedom. Fear had overtaken them. They feared being punished by Pharaoh for having believed in the word of the Lord that came through Moses. In their unbelief they felt foolish for having believed God loved them enough to bring them out of slavery into a place of freedom and completeness. They did not understand the process. They wanted the provision of the promise, but not the process! They did not like being in the crucible of faith.

They had not understood, like many Christians today, that the provision of God's promise is conditional: we have to put off our old ways of thinking and believing and believe and trust in God's word (His promise) no matter what the circumstances. As Israel stood on the brink of yet another miracle, with Pharaoh fast approaching, they were being offered an opportunity to be delivered not just from their physical slave masters, but also their "stinking thinking" which kept them in spiritual bondage and slavery. This pressure point was affording them the chance to kick the habitual belief patterns that prevented them from receiving God's very best for their lives. Look at the difference between Moses' view of the situation and their own:

"And Moses said to the people, 'Do not be afraid. Standstill, and see the salvation of the Lord, which He will accomplish for you today. For the Egyptians whom you see today, you shall see again no more forever. The Lord will fight for you, and you shall hold your peace." (Exodus 14:11-14)

Here is a man just like them, in the same situation, facing the same fears, yet he doesn't see things the way the rest of the people do and he uses a completely different vocabulary! The people's attitude was that the Lord had brought them this far to leave them stranded and even kill them. Moses' attitude was: since the Lord has done all these miracles to bring us this far, He will not abandon us now! Moses fully expected God to do an even greater miracle and cut off their slave masters forevermore!

And so He did. One of the greatest miracles recorded in the Bible happens right there in the midst of their challenge. In obedience to the Lord, Moses dips his staff into the Red Sea and it begins to open up, providing Israel a way out of captivity. God's people march through the sea on dry land and, as they exit the sea, so Pharaoh and his army enter into the pathway created by the miracle. Moses raises his staff over the Red Sea and it begins to close again, drowning Pharaoh and his army. The people of God are free from the land of slavery. But God's ultimate plan for their future and freedom is not yet complete. They have another step to take.

Bitter or better?

You would think this group of people would be ecstatic at being free. They have experienced miracle after miracle. But, when they come to their first obstacle in the wilderness, the bitter waters of Marah, once again they reveal that you can be free from slavery on the outside, but unchanged on the inside. Their thinking was still "stinking"! They still possessed a "slave mentality" and it would be the ruin of them yet. We can be healthy and yet still talk and act like we are sick. We can prosper materially, but be bankrupt of spirit. We can be loved unconditionally, but still live a life controlled by rejection and self-pity. Yes, we can be free but still think and live like a slave.

Some two to three million people were now gathered in the wilderness of Shur needing a drink of water. The Lord's provision for them was an oasis, but the water was bitter to the taste. They named that place *Marah* meaning "bitter". What looked refreshing and exactly what they needed was in fact unpalatable. Once again we see the same pattern revealed: God's way forward and His answer to our prayers sometimes doesn't look or taste good to us! How can a bitter pool of water be a blessing? Once again the people began complaining to Moses. Their instant response to the situation was to be negative, rather than trust in God's wisdom. They still had no concept that God could turn such bitter experiences sweet for them.

"And the people complained against Moses, saying, 'What shall we drink?' So he cried out to the Lord, and the Lord showed him a tree. When he cast it into the waters, the waters were made sweet. There He made a statute and an ordinance for them. And there He tested them, and said, 'If you diligently heed the voice of the Lord your God and do what is right in His sight, give ear to His commandments and keep all His statutes, I will put none of the diseases on you which I have brought on the Egyptians. For I am the Lord who heals you.'" (Exodus 15:24-26)

One again it took the intervention and intercession of Moses to still their storm. The Lord instructed him to uproot a small tree and throw it into the water. Once it struck the waters they became sweet and the people were able to drink. The Hebrew word translated "tree" in this passage literally means, "tree, carpenter or gallows". When connected together, these concepts give us, *"a carpenter's son who hung upon a tree* (Galatians 3:13). The tree Moses cast on the water represented the cross of Calvary that Jesus used to turn our bitter experience of sin into a life of discovering how sweet it is to be loved by Him.

God was not concerned simply with providing the people a much needed drink to quench their thirst, He wanted to heal the diseases that were rampant in their bodies through living as slaves in Egypt. He had, and always has, the "bigger picture" in mind. Situations God allows us to experience are not just meant to deal with our immediate issues, they are designed to deal with the long term issues that reign in our belief system and thought patterns that will keep us from walking in the fullness of His promises.

How great is my God?

I remember the Lord speaking to me very clearly in late 1988, telling me He wanted me to take my family to South Africa to attend a conference and minister in some churches. I had known for several years that the Lord would one day open a door for me to go to South Africa, and now I had an opportunity to go. I had no idea how much it would cost for us all to go, however, so I called a Christian Travel agency and talked it over with them. After a while I heard the agent quietly announce the total price for the four of us to fly to South Africa: £2,200. My church was still so small at that time that my weekly income was £50. You can do the math yourself and see that there was no way I could afford to take this trip.

The agent asked me if I wanted him to book the flights and I responded, "Yes." Just to clarify here: I thought this meant he was going to *hold* the flights for me for a time, so I could think things over. I didn't realize he was asking me if I wanted him to *buy* the flights until I heard the words that sent a shiver through my whole being: "Okay sir, that's four tickets purchased for you. You have

five days to send the deposit and four weeks to pay the balance."
I was stunned into silence. The deposit was £600. I broke into a
cold sweat as I realized I had committed us to go and had no
money to pay for anything, let alone four tickets to fly to South
Africa. I felt sick to my stomach and after I hung up the phone I
ran straight to my prayer closet for help. There in the presence of
God I felt His peace wash over me and restore to me the peace I
was missing because of the panic that had entered my soul.

The panic stemmed from my guilt of having "done something
wrongly". I'd always had major difficulties in handling finances
and was terrified of making a mistake. I panicked thinking of the
consequences of not being able to pay for the tickets. My guilt
had produced in me a fear of punishment. There in my bedroom
the Holy Spirit began to show me that His love for me was greater
than any mistake I could make and that He had already delivered
me from the spirit of fear and guilt through the blood that Jesus
shed for me at Calvary. I came out of that room with a peace so
deep within my soul that I just knew God would provide a way
for us to do this great thing that was so impossible for me.

That afternoon one of my friends, a local pastor, called by to see
me and handed me an envelope. He had been praying and he and
his wife felt led by God to give us a financial gift of a few hundred
pounds. He said to me simply, "The Lord has told me to give you
this gift because *He wants you to go*. I don't know where you're
supposed to go, but He told me to tell you: 'Yes, go!'" Having
handed me the envelope he rushed off, leaving me wanting to
burst into tears of humility and gratitude or run round the house
shouting praises to God for His answer.

The next day there was a knock at our front door and I left my
study to go and answer it, only to find no one there. There was an
envelope on the doormat. Inside the envelope was £600. In the
space of two days, God had given me what would have taken me

twelve months to earn. I had our deposit and more.

Over the next few days a further £1,600 was given to us towards our trip. I was strutting around almost arrogantly saying to myself, "This *faith* thing is easy!" I was telling everyone how faithful God was and how trusting Him was the best thing to do. Then, (there is always a *then!*) I received a bill in the post that came out of nowhere. Can you guess how much it was for? Yes, exactly £1,600. I had in my hands the money needed for the balance of our airfares, but here was a bill to wipe out the whole lot. My heart sank desperately low. I tried hard to convince myself that the money we had been given was to buy our tickets to South Africa, but in my heart I knew the Lord was asking me to have integrity and pay the bill.

But can I believe He will do it again?

I began to get angry with the Lord and tell Him, "It's just not fair. You build up my hopes to go to South Africa and then take it all away! You're no different than anyone else. Everyone promises me something and then takes it away or lets me down!" God quietly waited for me to calm down and apologize to Him for my attitude. This was one of those divinely inspired moments He'd planned for my life and He was not about to miss this opportunity to deliver me from my "stinking thinking". He showed me that my fear and anger stemmed from wrong thinking. i.e. that if I paid the bill, God might not be willing to provide all the money a second time. The "unexpected" bill was, after all, my fault. It had appeared "out of nowhere" because I'd not managed our finances well. How could God just overlook that? I felt sure He would not now bless me financially, since I'd made a mess of things. But I had made the mistake of believing that God would only bless me if I was perfect.

I repented of my unbelief and asked for God's grace to help me believe in His goodness. I then gathered my family together in the kitchen for a talk. We stood in a circle and I told them what had happened and that I believed God was about to perform another financial miracle so that we could go to South Africa. The four of us began to sing in the spirit and praise God for His loving-kindness. We sang and sang at the top of our voices and suddenly, just like in the upper room on the day of Pentecost, the breath of God entered that room and filled us with His presence and power. We looked at each other with eyes beaming. At that moment each of us felt as though we were about to fly. We felt as if we were already aboard God's private airliner about to be transported to South Africa! What an unforgettable moment in our lives.

The next two weeks became a lesson of discovering that God's goodness is greater than my failures, weaknesses or abilities. Money poured in from everywhere and just a few weeks later we landed in South Africa for three weeks that would forever change our lives.

Storms are just distractions

When an eagle sees a storm approaching it does not fly in the opposite direction, it actually flies directly towards the storm. This is not the most logical or natural thing for a person to do when facing the storms of life – unless, that is, we understand what the eagle has to teach us.

During a storm, currents of warm air push upwards within it. These are thermals. The eagle has the ability to stretch out his wings and allow these warm air currents to lift him up. When he has a thermal under his wings he does not have to work hard to fly, he just has to tilt his wings slightly and the air does all the hard work while he simply glides. Studies of eagles have revealed that they can fly up to twice their normal speed and reach previously uncharted heights during a storm. The eagle can go faster, fly higher and see further, all because it turns the storm to its advantage. That's why it never flies away from one! It has learned that storms can propel it forward much quicker than calm air.

Similarly, all the major characters in the Bible faced storms of one sort or another which God turned to their advantage:

Abram and Sarai lived for many years believing for a son, but they could not conceive. Yet, when Abram was one hundred years old and Sarai ninety-nine years old – well beyond the age of conception by their own power – the Lord blessed them with a "faith son" by His supernatural ability.

David, who was rejected by his father and brothers for seventeen years and later persecuted by king Saul, was given the rule of the kingdom through patience and faith.

Joseph, another man who was despised by his brothers because he had favor with his father, was left for dead in a pit, brought into slavery, accused of raping his master's wife, wrongfully imprisoned and much more! But he waited, trusted God, and eventually became not only the second most powerful man in Egypt, but the one who was able to provide and protect Israel from death due to famine. His whole family prospered because he prospered.

Jesus was crucified in agony, totally rejected by all men when He had lived a perfect life and loved His neighbor as Himself. Yet the agony turned into jubilation. What looked bad turned out to be the most wonderful event creation has ever known. The list goes on and on.

The "donkey" that can carry you from your Bethany to your Jerusalem might not necessarily look "good" or like a blessing from God. Often it will look like it came directly from Hell and it will kick and hurt you like any donkey. But nevertheless, God can and will use it to transport you into the fullness of His blessing for your life.

Jesus' disciples were about to be rocked by the greatest storm imaginable. All they had trusted in, sacrificed for and built their hopes upon, was seemingly about to crumble and fall apart right in front of their eyes. They would be powerless to control the events about to unfold. So Jesus was giving them an illustrative sermon of how to handle the "donkey". He was showing them that storms come and storms go. We either ride them or we are drowned by them. Likewise, we can get kicked by our "donkey" or we can learn to ride it!

CHAPTER 11

THE UNUSUAL TUTOR ~ DAY 1

When the Lord answers our prayer for breakthrough He usually does it through a vehicle we are not expecting Him to use. The donkey the Lord provided for Jesus was a virgin donkey. It had never been used this way before. When the Lord appeared to Moses at the burning bush, He had never manifested Himself that way before. When He delivered Noah from the floods, He had never told anyone to build an ark before, nor had people ever encountered a flood before. When it was Elijah's time to make the transition to Heaven and Elisha's time to become the minister God had determined him to be, the Lord used a chariot of fire to separate them and lift Elijah into another realm. Where in the Bible do we see God ever do this again? Israel prayed for their Messiah to come. When He came, He came in a way and at a time such that they did not recognize Him and therefore missed their day of visitation and salvation.

Over and over again this is a pattern that God uses when bringing transition into the life of His people. Yet people who have seen God move in past times and are praying for a fresh move of God, can end up becoming the very ones who fight against the new move when it arrives. Why? Because it didn't happen the way they thought it would. They did not recognize it was the Lord answering their prayer.

In chapter 7 we looked at the example of Mary discovering Jesus' empty tomb. She saw a person she perceived was a gardener, when it was in fact Jesus. How did she not recognize Him? After all, she had dedicated her life to serving and following Him! It was because Jesus had *changed*. Mary was so busy looking for that which she'd always known that she ran past a living, breathing Jesus looking for a dead one!

Such events are *virgin* experiences for God's people to handle. The donkeys God sends into our lives are "mentors" to enable us to make our transitions. We can kick against them or learn to ride them into our destiny like Jesus did.

Transparency precedes transition

God's Word clearly confirms that within us we have a measure of untapped life in God that is above and beyond that which we could ever imagine. It supersedes our wildest dreams, but lies dormant or is under-utilized for most of our lives, waiting to be drawn upon and lived in. The "unfinished business" in our lives so often becomes the blockage that stops this river flowing. The moment we are healed and the blockages removed, the river of God begins to flow in and through us in ways we had been hoping and praying for years.

The moment Jesus begins to ride His donkey something amazing takes place around Him. Spontaneously, people begin to take off their garments. They throw them onto the donkey or to the floor and collectively burst into praise and rejoicing. They are celebrating. When you desire to leave your "Bethany" there has to be a disclosure, an uncovering, a casting aside of that which keeps you tied to it. When we have dealt with those things that tie us to our past or present experiences or prevent us from moving on, there comes a release of inward joy as we celebrate our new-found freedom and healing, followed by an outward expression of the newness of His kind of life.

It is our old habits, attitudes, belief systems and unhealed internal wounds that keep us tied firmly to our past or present. We try so hard to change and break free in order to have a different experience or lifestyle, but life never seems to change. We seem to go around in circles, visiting the same experiences and pains over and over again and this culminates in anger and frustration as we fail to control our life. We become resentful at others who seem to be living the life we have always desired to live. We become disillusioned with ourselves, our life and God, believing that if He really loved us He would do something about the situation – when all along He is!

No one experiences a major life change or breakthrough without experiencing the pain that causes them to search for the answers to their situation and make the necessary adjustments in order for that change to happen. The "truth" that has the power to set us free, first has the power to hurt us. No pain, no gain!

Laying aside the foliage

The crowd gathers and increases in size as Jesus and His disciples begin their journey. This clearly shows us that when we make the steps of faith and obedience the Lord asks us to make and we overcome the opposition to our faith, it has an impact on everyone around us. Those who also desire to break free in areas of their lives are drawn to us. People were drawn to Jesus from everywhere and joined the procession from bondage to freedom, from brokenness and lack to wholeness and abundance in all things.

People had taken off their outer garments and thrown them onto the floor so that the donkey could walk over them. But now the crowd were stripping branches from the trees along the way to do the same thing. We will see later that just twenty-four hours after this event, Jesus goes to a fig tree to look for fruit on it, but the tree is covered in foliage. It has no fruit on it because it is not the season for fruit! So here are a multitude of people tearing down branches that have foliage but no fruit on them. We noted earlier that Adam and Eve covered themselves with leaves from a fig tree after they sinned. God had declared that His creative works were *"very good"* (Genesis 1:12;31), so Adam and Eve covered themselves with a covering of good works, hoping God would be pleased next time He saw them. But they had not removed the sin they had committed, just covered over it!

Look at the following scriptures about being fruitful:

*"And let our people also learn to maintain good works, to meet urgent needs, that they may not be **unfruitful.**"* (Titus 3:14)

*"And even now the axe is laid to the root of the trees. Therefore every tree which does not bear good **fruit** is cut down and thrown into the fire."* (Matthew 3:10)

*"Every tree that does not bear good **fruit** is cut down and thrown into the fire. Therefore by their **fruits** you will know them."* (Matthew 7:19-20)

God is more concerned with us bearing fruit than foliage. Fruit is the evidence that the tree is reproducing its internal life. Each fruit carries seeds within itself – the ability to reproduce itself. The Bible shows clearly that trees represent people. Like a tree we can have lots of foliage – be involved in all kinds of activities that look good – and yet not produce fruit i.e. we are not reproducing the life of the Holy Spirit who dwells within us. The fruit of the Spirit are listed in Galatians 5:22:

"But the fruit of the Spirit is love, joy, peace, longsuffering, kindness, goodness, faithfulness, gentleness, self-control." (Galatians 5:22-23)

As Christians we are not simply called to go to church, be good people and be nice and kind to others. We are to allow the Holy Spirit to live His life through us and reveal the likeness of Christ to our world. We are to preach His Gospel and bring people to salvation, lay hands on the sick and see them healed, cast out demons, and bring release and a new freedom to those who are bound up in fear, hurt or grief because of the traumatic events they have experienced. These are the fruit and evidence that He dwells in us, that we are growing and changing from glory to glory. I don't desire to go to Heaven and hear the Lord say, "Well done, Wynne," only to discover that I walked in just 10% of the power and authority of God I could have walked in. I don't want to have accomplished only 10% of what was possible for me to accomplish. Jesus died that I might live in 100% of what He purchased for me to live in. This is my goal in life: to do 100% of all He says I can do; to live in *100%* of what He purchased for me to live in; to not experience 100% of what He died to protect me from. That's fruitfulness.

For us to move from our "Bethany" or "Bethphage" to "Jerusalem" the Holy Spirit will lead us to lay down those areas of our life that are all activity and no fruitfulness. He doesn't desire us to live a Christian life where we look busy for Jesus, but if someone were to move away the leaves on the surface they would find no fruit.

In John 15:1-5 Jesus says,

"I am the true vine, and My Father is the vinedresser. Every branch in Me that does not bear fruit He takes away; and every branch that bears fruit He prunes, that it may bear more fruit. You are already clean because of the word which I have spoken to you. Abide in Me, and I in you. As the branch cannot bear fruit of itself, unless it abides in the vine, neither can you, unless you abide in Me. I am the vine, you are the branches. He who abides in Me, and I in him, bears much fruit; for without Me you can do

nothing."

Every good gardener knows that a tree or bush with loads of foliage but no fruit needs to be pruned. So he/she cuts away the unnecessary branches that distract the plant from producing fruit. Better to have fewer branches and fruit, than lots of branches covered with foliage protruding everywhere, but no fruit. The gardener is not hurting the plant, in fact just the reverse! The gardener can see its potential and knows that afterwards the plant will look magnificent. Often pruning needs to be severe and sometimes it can look as though the plant will never recover from the pruning. But the next year the plant will be full of fruit. So it is with God, our Gardener.

At the beginning of every year we should lay down our activities, our plans and our lifestyle before God and ask for His wisdom and guidance for the year ahead. There may be areas that He desires to alter (trim) or even ask us to stop (cut off altogether). No matter how painful these requests may be, they are always for our good.

He takes a good look around

After they have traveled for seven miles Jesus and His disciples arrive at Jerusalem. The disciples were, I believe, much more like us in our churches today than we like to think. The size of the crowd, their jubilation, the intensity of their praises, the crowds calling Jesus the "Son of David" all convince the disciples that *this* visit to Jerusalem will be a memorable one.

Jesus was a man of great order and delegation. He had trained His disciples well over three and a half years. He had taught them how to handle the crowds, how to release the anointing, and how to recognize the prophetic voice of God their heavenly Father. He had shown them all they needed to see. Each had a job and function in His team. Jesus did not function like some churches I know who believe if you organize a meeting it will stifle the moving of the Holy Spirit.

Judas was the treasurer! Others were ones who went ahead of the team preparing their accommodation and food. Others accompanied Jesus during personal times of ministry or intercession. He divided them all into teams to preach and also to distribute the loaves and fishes.

I believe that as Jesus approached Jerusalem His team began to think of the meetings, the crowds, the offerings, the miracles and everything else that happened at the BIG events! (Jesus' team today would have included a Sound Technician, a Road Manager and a Resources Manager handling His CD/Mp3 of the month and His latest books and DVDs! And let's not forget the TV crew!)

Each person would have been thinking of their own area of responsibility, planning what they would have to get done when the team arrived at Jerusalem. Judas would no doubt have loved the offering times in Jerusalem. The crowds would have been large! So he presumed that the offerings would be also. The ushers would have been concerned about how to control the crowds who so passionately loved to press in on Jesus. The sound department would have been looking to see where was the best place to erect the stage and the PA system to get the best sound for the meetings. (I know Jesus didn't have some of these things. I am just trying to help you picture it in a contemporary context!)

As Jesus arrived at Jerusalem His team would have burst into action planning the meetings. Jesus walked off and went into the Temple leaving them to it. The Bible says He had a good look around in the Temple then simply turned and walked out, heading back to Bethany. The disciples, busy with their preparations, were caught off guard, surprised that He had headed out of the city without any warning. No doubt one of them asked Him where He was going. "Back to Bethany," came the simple response without one word of explanation.

The disciples looked at one another in disbelief. "What, no meetings Lord?" cried out one of them. Jesus just gestured to them to stop what they were doing and follow Him. They hastily packed away everything in order to catch up with Him, questioning why Jesus would walk all the way to Jerusalem in the heat of the day, just to take a look around in the Temple and promptly head back the seven miles to Bethany. Jesus said not a word to explain His actions.

You are the temple of God

"Do you not know that you are the temple of God and that the Spirit of God dwells in you?" (1 Corinthians 3:16)

Could it be that Jesus was trying to show them that when the Lord brings transition into our lives, it is preceded by the Holy Spirit looking deep into our hearts to prepare us for what He is about to do – for it is our heart that controls our life.

*"Keep your **heart** with all diligence, for out of it spring the issues of life."* (Proverbs 4:23)

The Lord instructed Israel to build Him a temple in Jerusalem so that He could dwell in the midst of His people. When Solomon finished building the temple, the Lord filled it with His glory and multitudes came from every nation on the earth to see this beautiful sight (2 Chronicles 5). When Jesus, who *is* the glory of God in its fullest form, visited the Temple it had become void of the glory, power and presence of God. It had become filled with the very things that prevented His glory residing there. Now, He was going to drive out from it the things that made it unclean and restore it to be the place of worship He had always intended it to be.

Biblical history shows time and time again that God raised up a leader who was a worshipper to return Israel to God. They always did it by cleansing the temple and restoring the true worship of God in it. When this happened God's presence could fill the land. In the same way Jesus was preparing Jerusalem for the greatest visitation of God they had ever known.

CHAPTER 12

DRIVING OUT THE THIEF – DAY 2

The next morning Jesus arises and beckons the disciples to follow Him again. "Where are we going today?" questions one of them. "Jerusalem," replies Jesus with a hint of a smile on His face. "JERUSALEM?" comes the loud response from His team. "But we went there yesterday, Lord," protests one of them, "and all you did was take a good look around and walk all the way back here to Bethany. Why go again? Nothing's changed. Things will be exactly as they were yesterday!" Jesus didn't give an explanation, He just headed towards the road for Jerusalem, leaving behind Him a room full of bemused faces looking at one another.

There are times when Jesus does not explain things to us. He is more interested in seeing if we are willing to follow Him, whether we understand or not. Many times Jesus taught by using parables, giving no explanation of their meaning. It was His way of making people search their hearts and look inside themselves for the meaning. Jesus would not always be with them physically to answer their questions, but the Holy Spirit would be within them and He could give them the revelation they needed. Giving no explanation made Jesus' disciples curious as to His motives and plans. It made them talk about it all day on the journey. It became a journey they would never forget, but it started as one that didn't make sense!

I am sure the disciples followed Jesus on these journeys muttering under their breath, complaining and sharing their opinions to one another just like congregations do today when the leadership of their church does something they don't expect or understand! Sometimes not understanding is the donkey – we just need to shut our mouths and follow!

The tree that bore no fruit

As they arrive at the brow of the Mount of Olives, Jesus motions to His team to pause and walks a short distance away to inspect a fig tree to see if there are any figs on it, because He is hungry. This has to be one of the most preached portions of the Bible, but seldom do I hear a preacher really grasp hold of the truths hidden beneath the narrative. We must really picture the faces of the disciples at this point. Peter has already had the revelation that Jesus is the Christ, the Son of the living God. They know He is the Messiah. They have followed Him for over three years seeing miracles, healings, deliverance's, signs and wonders. They also know that the One standing in front of them was raised in the same country and region as them. He knows what time of year it is. He knows when it is the season for figs. He is not stupid! He is the One who, by the power of His spoken word, made the universe, the earth, the sun, light, rain, and the ground the tree stands in! He created the fig tree, giving it the ability it has to reproduce itself. He is also the One who created the season for it to bear fruit. Don't you think He knew it was not the time or season for figs? Could it be that His hunger was not for physical fruit, but for spiritual fruit to come into the lives of His disciples? Was Jesus perhaps using this tree to reveal to His disciples a spiritual truth that they had not yet understood?

Where there's a fruit, there's a root

"So He took the blind man by the hand and led him out of the town. And when He had spit on his eyes and put His hands on him, He asked him if he saw anything. And he looked up and said, 'I see men like trees, walking.'" (Mark 8:23-24)

To my remembrance this is the only occasion the New Testament says that Jesus prayed for the same person twice before He saw the miracle. For it to be included in the writings of the apostles it must have made an incredible impact upon them. I believe it's included in Scripture because there is another spiritual truth behind this event that we must also learn on our journey of transition.

If, as stated earlier, it is our heart that orders our life, then Jesus must first heal us on the inside before we see a manifestation of that healing on the outside. I find it remarkable that Jesus prays for this man and then steps back and asks him to describe what he sees. He doesn't ask him if he can see, but what he sees. Jesus had no doubt the man would be healed, so why ask him this question? Once again, are we getting a glimpse into the spiritual dimension through Jesus' actions?

"He shall be like a tree planted by the rivers of water, that brings forth its fruit in its season, whose leaf also shall not wither; and whatever he does shall prosper". (Psalm 1:3)

"That they may be called trees of righteousness, the planting of the Lord, that He may be glorified." (Isaiah 61:3)

"Even so, every good tree bears good fruit, but a bad tree bears bad fruit. A good tree cannot bear bad fruit, nor can a bad tree bear good fruit ... Therefore by their fruits you will know them." (Matthew 7:17-20)

Throughout the Bible people are depicted as trees. The Bible shows that God's work with man began and revolved around trees in a garden. The book of Revelation ends centered around the Tree of Life. In the middle, as it were, Jesus deals with all of man's problems by allowing God the Father to nail Him to a tree.

A tree has roots, a trunk, foliage and fruit. A seed is planted in the unseen realm of the soil and ends up producing fruit in the visible realm. Remember this one truth: wherever you see a fruit there must be a root! If you want to eliminate the fruit on a tree you don't pick the fruit, you lay an axe to the root. If you pick the fruit from a tree it merely sends a message to the infrastructure of the tree to produce more fruit. If you "dead head" flowers on a bush, the bush instantly tries to replace the flowers that have died. You can keep a bush flowering for longer by removing the old flowers.

To me, a gardening novice, many trees look the same. But if I wish to identify a tree all I have to do is to inspect the fruit. Two trees may look similar, but the fruit clearly separates them and makes identification easy. Once you identify the fruit, you instantly know what the root is! If there is bad fruit on the tree and you desire to get rid of it, you must deal with the problem which is in the roots. The tree derives its life from the soil and its roots.

Many people have come to me over my years of pastoring and told me about the problems in their lives, marriages, families, work or finances. Nearly always these people thought their problem was the physical issue or situation they were encountering. They didn't understand that their problem was not what was occurring in the visible realm, but in the unseen realm of their heart. Debt, sickness, divorce, arrogance, anger and the inability to keep relationships can be the result of wrong seeds planted in a person's heart. Words and actions are spiritual forces, not merely the physical outworking of a person's life. When wrong words and actions pierce the heart (the soil) they root themselves more firmly than any earthly tree. Eventually those seeds will mature and become a tree that bears "fruit" through a person's life. We can try as hard as we can to break free, but we won't unless we dig up the roots and stop their force from flowing in our life.

Could it be that when Jesus prayed for the blind man He was showing us the way to true healing was to understand this principle? When we can see clearly that our life is like a tree and we begin to deal with issues from the inside out, instead of the outside in, then the greatest healing of all is taking place.

Honor your father and mother

"Honor your father and your mother, as the Lord your God has commanded you, that your days may be long, and that it may be well with you in the land which the Lord your God is giving you." (Deuteronomy 5:16)

A number of years ago I had a serious financial problem. I was the fifth generation of my family to live in poverty, but God brought me to a place where I understood He wanted me to break free of debt and poverty and reverse that curse in my life – not just for myself, but for the generations who would follow. But no matter how I tried to break through and find victory over my finances, I just kept failing and it seemed I was getting in a worse situation the more I strived to get out of it. I tithed everything that came into my house. I gave to missions. I prayed over my offerings, thanking God for His blessing on my finances. I would occasionally even put my check book on the floor and dance around, praising God and confessing His Word over my situation! But still I couldn't break free.

Sometimes I am still so much like a Pharisee. I can do all the right things and believe God will bless me because of my external actions. But external religion burdens you and discourages you. I became so despondent. I felt like a failure because I couldn't get victory over my debt. In desperation I decided to enter a three-day complete fast. I knew God's Word showed clearly that He desires all people to prosper, so the problem wasn't that He was holding out on me – it had to be something on my part that needed dealing with. I just couldn't see what!

Within moments of me beginning to pray on my first day of prayer and fasting, the Lord spoke clearly to me. What leapt into my spirit was the verse quoted above about honoring our father and mother. It seemed such a strange thing to come into my mind at that point that I ignored it and carried on praying. Then it came a second time. "Why does this verse keep coming to me?" I thought. I couldn't see it was connected to my prayer direction at all, so I pushed it aside once more. For three long days I fasted and prayed. It was so hard to concentrate. I struggled to go without food, when in the past I had not found it a problem. It seemed as if the Lord wasn't in what I was doing. Worse still, at the end of three days I had not heard the voice of the Lord nor received any wisdom of the Spirit. Or so it seemed!

I cried out to the Lord in desperation. I wanted so much to know what to do. Immediately that verse of scripture came to me a third time. "What does that have to do with my financial problem?" I cried to God. Then, as I read it slowly, I began to see the connection to a heart issue in the unseen realm that was effecting the visible realm of my life. I had a great relationship with my mother, but my relationship with my father was not great. Maybe I had not honored him as I should? Real honor comes from the heart. We can say all the right words on the outside, convincing everyone that we are a respectful person, but God knows the difference between heartfelt honor and lip service. One is truth, the other is just religion.

I wanted to be a good Christian son to the Lord and to obey Him, even if I didn't fully understand how this affected my financial situation. I remember calmly talking to the Lord, asking Him how He would like me to honor my father. "Shall I buy him a shirt and tie, or maybe a suit? Or perhaps take him out for a meal?" The next words I heard took my breath away and almost made my heart leap out of my chest: "Go tell your father that you love him!" There was no point in saying anything, I knew it was the Lord. Silence filled my prayer closet, but the noise within me was deafening. A contradictory voice began screaming at me that it wasn't God who had said these words. The voice of logic began to express its opinion. Disrespect began to try to get my attention and remind me of my father's failures, saying that he didn't deserve my respect. But louder than all these other voices was the one that got my attention the most: it was the voice of my fear of rejection.

I could go and obey the Lord and tell my father that I loved him, but how would I cope if he turned round and ridiculed me, ignored me or told me he didn't love me? How would I cope with facing my biggest fear: the fear of not being significant to him? It took days for me to come to terms with what the Lord had said. Eventually though, I went to visit my parents. My heart pounded as I entered their house, my mother instantly noticing the perspiration running down the side of my face. She said nothing about it, but just handed me a drink. I slowly faced up to the task of talking to my father and headed for the sitting room.

He took one look at me and asked, "What's the matter?" Isn't it amazing how parents can read us like a book! "Nothing," my voice squeaked through nervousness. How does a 34-year old son say for the first time to his father, "Dad, I love you!" I had no recollection of him ever telling me he loved me. As a father he had never harmed me, but neither had he been demonstrative or affectionate with me.

He asks us to do the impossible

Each time I tried to say the words my tongue glued itself to the roof of my mouth. I left the room and returned to the kitchen where my mother was cooking. She could see I was in a worse state than when I'd arrived. "What's the matter?" she asked quietly. I just pretended everything was fine. I tried once again to talk to my father, each time leaving the room a little worse than the last time. Three times in all I tried to tell my father that I loved him, but I couldn't cross that line of fear. In a mixture of frustration and condemnation I raced out of the house, got in my car and returned home. I cried and shouted all at the same time: "I can't do this! It's too hard. If you want me to do it, then you'll just have to do it through me, because I can't do it!" Peace flooded my heart instantly, as if I knew I had just said the words that the Lord had been waiting for years for me to say. He knew I couldn't do it and wanted me to understand this. He was trying to teach me that He wanted to live His life *through* me. Only by letting Him do this would I ever see the supernatural life of God flow through me in an immeasurable way.

Months went by and I totally forgot what had happened until one evening when the phone rang while we were busy clearing up after a meal. It was my mother who, through sobbing, was quietly trying to tell me that my father had been very poorly. The doctor had examined him and concluded that he may only have days to live. Hastily, my family and I went to see him. We all sat around his bed as he struggled to stay awake. I had never seen him as frail as this and I was struggling to hold back the tears. My little children eventually went off to play, followed a little while later by Anne slipping out of the room, sensing the need for my father and I to be alone.

We talked about many different things until the Lord reminded me that I was not only his son, but a minister of the Gospel of Jesus and I needed to ask my father if he was ready to meet Him. My father had attended a Methodist church all of his life. He had always been the choirmaster and one of the "pillars" of the church. But for all his involvement he would never sit and talk about the Lord. He would either leave the room or end up arguing over some religious topic. It was as if he couldn't talk about the Lord in a personal way.

My father assured me that he was happy to meet Jesus if this was his moment. I quietly asked him to tell me why he could be so confident. To my surprise he began to tell me that he had made a decision to ask Jesus into his life when he was just a teenager. He shared with me how it had impacted him so much that he would stand in the streets and outside the coal mines to preach to people as they traveled back and forth from work. I was staggered. I had never heard of this part of his life. Eagerly I got him to talk about it more, finally discovering that he had felt called to the ministry.

A tear began to run down his cheek as he told me of a terrible event that had happened between him and his stepfather. As a boy he had been repeatedly sexually abused by this man. The deep pain of this trauma scarred him so badly that he became filled with bitterness and unforgiveness. It also made him wonder why, if God really loved him, He had not intervened. Slowly, through the hurt and the questions, his passion for Jesus died. He had then spent all of his life going through the rituals of church attendance without joy and peace, all because of unresolved anger and unforgiveness towards his stepfather. There in the vulnerability of the moment he asked me to pray with him. As we held hands he prayed a prayer of forgiveness. He forgave his stepfather and then asked the Lord to forgive him for holding bitterness in his heart towards him for all these years.

Now truly exhausted he knew he needed to sleep, but I didn't want him to. I was afraid he would never wake up. For the first time in my life I felt close to my father and I was afraid this was about to be snatched from me. But it was pointless trying to keep him awake, so I promised I would be there for him the moment he woke up. He squeezed my hand and with tears in his eyes again, he thanked me for being me, for the talk and for praying with him.

Without even thinking, I instinctively leaned over, kissed him on the lips, and out of my mouth came the words that my spirit had been waiting for thirty-four years for me to utter: "Dad, I love you."

As I said the words I broke into floods of tears and began to sob and sob from the depths of my being. He put his arms around me and began to kiss me over and over, saying, "Son, I love you too." It probably wasn't very long, but it felt like we were crying for hours. We cried out the tears of pain and disappointment we had both buried for years. The great news was that my father lived another twelve years! God had tricked me and I had received my breakthrough!

So, you see, what started off looking like it was going to be a painful event to deal with, turned out to be one of the greatest moments of my entire life. From that moment on, day after day, I would visit my father and tell him I loved him so much and he would say it to me in return. We talked freely about the Lord now his guilty conscience had been healed and freed. And without trying, suddenly both he and I began to prosper financially. All through his life he and my mother had struggled financially, yet here he was prospering, all because he had forgiven and honored his father in the eyes of God and the same had happened to me.

Deal with the log-jams

I share this testimony often as I preach around the world and I have had the privilege of praying with countless thousands of men who, like me, have had the same experience with their fathers. Some of the greatest miracles and healings I have seen in my ministry have happened as men forgave and honored their fathers, even seeking them out to tell them that they loved them. Both men and women have written to me to tell me that after hearing this message and applying it to their lives, it has saved their marriage and their family. When we have "unfinished business" in our heart, the love and life of God that resides within us is prevented from flowing out to others, stifling our relationships in so many different ways.

Men have often told me they were unable to be really close to their children, struggling to be affectionate. Others told me they were not affectionate and gentle with their wives, leaving their wives feeling unfulfilled and with a sense of loneliness. All of this because of unfinished business with a father.

Women have shared with me that their father physically or sexually abused them and how this left them being almost sexually frigid towards their husband as they struggled to respect, honor and trust the man in their lives who had done them no harm at all. All of this because they allowed the pain of their experience to lodge as an offence within their heart. But I am so thankful to see and hear of so many wonderful healings and breakthroughs as people deal with the log-jams of their hearts in this way.

"There are no figs!"

When Jesus arrived at the fig-tree, He lifted the leaves on the tree and then shouted out so the disciples could hear, "There are no figs!' The Bible says He had walked 100 yards from them to where the tree was. He would need to shout quite loudly for them to hear. Why would He do this, when all He needed to do was to return to them and inform them the tree was fruitless?

They probably shouted back to Him, "We could have told you that! You didn't need to walk over to the tree to find that out. It's not the right season for figs!"

But then Jesus really blows their minds and speaks to the tree so loudly that they can hear Him cursing the tree. Remember to picture this from the disciples' point of view. Here is the man they have placed their trust in. They have left homes, businesses and families to follow Him. They have proclaimed to everyone that He is the Messiah everyone in Israel has been praying for. They believe He is the Son of God. And now He is talking to trees?

I can imagine their faces at this point! They are probably dumbstruck with their mouths open wide. They are probably wondering if the pressure is getting to Jesus. Is He cracking under the strain? Talking to trees? They thought it was crazy. Yet, He was teaching them to unleash the greatest weaponry in their spiritual armor. He was asking them to *step over* and leave behind all they had been taught during their upbringing and *step into* a brand new arena for the next level of their life and ministry. He was teaching them the power of the spoken word. He knew that if they could just believe they would understand and see that God's Word coming out of their mouth was as powerful as when it comes out of God's mouth! This lesson of Jesus did not make sense to the disciples right now, but in just a few hours they would understand it perfectly.

He walked back to the disciples and they probably continued their journey to Jerusalem in silence. Jesus was breaking down the walls of their deeply held concepts and understanding.

You can't earn His blessings!

As Jesus entered the Temple courtyards He stopped and asked for a large stick and some leather. He sat quietly on the steps and began to construct a whip. At first the disciples had no idea what He was making, then all of a sudden it became clear to them that He was making a whip. Why would he need a whip? Despite a history of hymns, carols, choruses and preacher's sermons, I wish to declare to you that "gentle Jesus, meek and mild" is nonsense! The Lamb of God is about to show that He is also the Lion of the

Tribe of Judah and He is a King who will attack and drive out anything that contaminates His Temple.

With stunned faces the disciples watch as Jesus kicks over the tables of money-lenders and drives out the people who are carrying their wares through the Temple, shouting for all to hear,

"Is it not written, 'My house shall be called a house of prayer for all nations'? But you have made it a 'den of thieves'." (Mark 11:17)

Of course, many have felt Jesus was teaching us not to sell and buy things in a church building. But I really don't think that is what He was doing at all. He described the people there as "thieves". In John 10:10 Jesus says that Satan, the devil, is a thief who comes to steal, kill and destroy. I believe He was saying to us that the activities happening in front of Him in the Temple are the very things that are *stealing* His presence and power from the Temple and the people of God. The thing that will separate them from the world around them is being stolen from them!

What was happening in front of Him? He saw money changers who were cheating and robbing ordinary people, so that the people who came to worship at the Temple went away worse off for their visit instead of better off! Everyone who came to Jesus sick, blind, demon possessed or hungry, went away healed, seeing, delivered and well fed! We should always come away happy and blessed from spending time in the presence of God. But these money lenders were making people worse off after visiting the House of God! As Christians, when we gather together in any place to worship God together, then we ought to return from that place strengthened, renewed in hope and faith, and full of His joy and life. We should not walk out of a church gathering more heavy laden than when we went in. We should be so happy and overflowing in His life that everyone around us is curious to find out where we have been, because the joy is written all over our face. Some people come away from church gatherings with faces looking as though they've been dipped in vinegar and lemon juice! Yet just hours prior to the meeting they were in some sporting arena jumping and shouting, expressing their joy and support for their team. Why should people feel intimidated or restrained in the presence of God, just because that's how "church" has always been done?

We don't need to provide church meetings that remind everyone how bad and destructive sin is, or how ungodly our society is becoming – we can read about it in any newspaper or turn on any television or radio news program to find it clearly portrayed. Instead, we need to hear the Gospel of Jesus preached with such passion, conviction and clarity that faith and hope arise in us. We need to be reminded that God lives in us by His Spirit and He will overcome the world through us. We have no need to be afraid. It is His joy to defeat sin, destroy guilt and remove fear from the lives of all who call upon His name and put their faith in Him. Miracles are easy – they are the byproduct of His abiding presence in our lives. They are normal to Jesus. They must become so in our life.

We don't need sermons that leave us flattened, defeated, guilt-ridden and with no hope that God can change anything. We need preachers that preach the fire of God back into us so we walk through our world destroying the works of darkness and setting captives free. This is real Church!

There were people buying and selling in the Temple. Others were carrying their wares through it. The word "wares" is an old English word for "products" or "goods for sale". We get the word "warehouse" from it. A warehouse is a place that houses "wares" and when we sell our wares we gain a profit or "earnings" from it. In other words, these people were more concerned with buying and selling their way into the presence of God than coming to Him empty-handed and calling on His mercy. The priests who were in charge of the Temple were sending the wrong message to the people. Without realizing it, they were making the people believe that they had to buy or earn their way into the presence and favor of God. What a disgusting lie to portray, that we could possibly buy our salvation, healing, miracles or entrance into Heaven. Of course, many preachers and churches have continued this horrendous lie even in our own times. If we could "buy" or "earn" our salvation or miracle, then why did Christ need to be crucified?

*"Whoever **calls** on the name of the* LORD *shall be saved."* (Romans 10:13)

*"For by **grace** you have been saved through faith, and that not of yourselves; it is the **gift** of God, not of **works**, lest anyone should boast."* (Ephesians 2:8)

The Bible says if we just "call" on Him we will be saved. We don't have to work or earn our salvation or blessing from God. Ephesians 2:8 says our salvation is a "gift" from Him. The Greek word do'ron is used by Paul the apostle for the word "gift". It means "a present ... a sacrifice". A present is a free gift from one person to another, it is not earned. A gift is another person showing us how much they love us and what they have sacrificed in order to give the gift to us. Paul is describing the immeasurable gift of forgiveness and salvation that God gives us through the great sacrifice of Jesus at Calvary.

The sacrifice of Jesus was a complete and sufficient sacrifice to redeem every man, woman and child, of *every* generation, from every sin and the consequences of that sin. We cannot add one thing to His freewill offering of His own life and blood. He paid the price for mankind's sin in full. If you or I try to "earn" or "work" for our salvation we are insinuating that we need to add something to it in order to make it work and we rub the perfect sacrifice of Jesus into the face of God and declare it was not enough.

This lie has kept millions out of Heaven and has prevented countless millions of miracles happening, because while we are trying to buy or earn our salvation we cannot receive it as a free gift! We receive everything from God by faith, not works! We can't earn, work for or become worthy enough to deserve what He gives us. We don't deserve it – that's just the point! We will never get to the place where we deserve it, so it *has* to be a *free gift*.

"He has appeared to put away sin by the sacrifice of Himself." (Hebrews 9:26)

*"For if by the one man's offense death reigned through the one, much more those who receive abundance of grace and of the **gift** of righteousness will reign in life through the one, Jesus Christ. Therefore, as through one man's offence judgment came to all men, resulting in condemnation, even so through one Man's righteous act the **free gift** came to all men, resulting in justification of life."* (Romans 5:17-18)

*"For if the blood of bulls and goats and the ashes of a heifer, sprinkling the unclean, sanctifies for the purifying of the flesh, how much more shall the blood of Christ, who through the eternal Spirit offered Himself without spot to God, cleanse your conscience from **dead works** to serve the living God?"* (Hebrews 9:13-14)

Silently, I would imagine, the disciples followed Jesus back over the Mount of Olives to Bethany that night stunned by this side of Jesus they had never seen before. Hour by hour, day by day, He was challenging their every concept, their image of God, their doctrine and revelation, but especially their faith, and all without telling them why.

It was physically dark as they passed over the crest of the mountain, but darker still within their souls I believe. Yet, it was the dawning of the greatest hour and day mankind has ever known. Presently the disciples could not see it, but within a few hours they would.

There is one thing I have learned in my years of walking with Jesus. The darker it seems to get and the more confusing life becomes, the closer we are than ever before to our breakthrough. We want God to reveal to us everything He is going to do, so that we can understand all that we are going through. That's because we have an inward drive to be "in control" of every situation. But instead we have to simply trust that He has all things under *His* control and that the outcome will always be for our good, not our harm.

CHAPTER 13

YOUR FINEST HOUR ~ DAY 3 PART 1

Early the next morning Jesus wakes His disciples to make the journey to Jerusalem for the third time. They no longer argue or complain about making the same journey three days running. They are probably still quieted by the events of the past two days. I think a deep sense of peace must have come into their hearts, despite all they were experiencing. Deep down they knew Jesus was the Messiah, the Son of God. They *knew* He could be trusted and that He wasn't going crazy. I believe they had a deep awareness He was about to do something that was going to be greater than anything they'd ever known.

You and I, if we have a real relationship with the Lord, experience times like this ourselves. Many times I have sensed the Lord is about to move in some powerful way before it happens. I have gone to church always believing we'll have a good time in the presence of the Lord, but all of a sudden, from somewhere within me comes an assertive assurance that the Holy Spirit will move in power and it will be a glorious meeting with people being healed. You just know it! We have a spirit that *knows* things before we *see* them with our natural eyes. This, I believe, is the sense the disciples had on their way out of Bethany and Bethphage on that third morning.

Christians all around the world right now are convinced in their hearts that we are about to experience the greatest demonstration of God's power and grace since the days Jesus walked on this earth. I do! I *know* that I *know* that I *know* we are about to see the greatest harvest of souls ever to come into the kingdom of God in one generation. I believe we are about to see the greatest explosion of miracles the world has ever seen. I believe we will see the greatest fulfillment of the Word of God we have ever known and all unfulfilled prophetic words will come to pass. And if I speak the truth, then within you, in your *knower*, you will believe the same! This is not a time to sleep spiritually. It is time to awaken to our finest hour.

The tree of life or death?

As Jesus led the disciples to the crest of the Mount of Olives He was interceding for them. It was time for them to understand the revelation and truth that had motivated Him to leave Heaven, be born of a virgin with humble beginnings, endure the ridicule and rejection of all men, including His disciples and friends, and gladly give Himself up to the torture and pain of Calvary.

He was praying that the Holy Spirit would give them eyes to see and ears to hear as they passed by the fig tree He had spoken to the day before. "Holy Spirit, let them see" He eagerly prayed over and over. Then suddenly, with a shout of hysteria, Peter screamed out, *"Rabbi* [teacher] *look! The fig tree which you cursed **has** withered away"* (v21). Everyone stopped and joined in the shouting in sheer amazement at what they could see with their eyes.

The disciples talked about the miracle. They discussed the amazing fact that Jesus kept demonstrating His power over creation. They talked about how they had doubted Him the day before, but *now* ... well, anything was possible. What He had spoken had come to pass and the tree had withered away.

Jesus did not wish for them simply to see another miracle or demonstration of His power. It was essential that they grasp the revelation behind His actions and this miracle. "Yes, Peter, yes, but what else do you see?" Jesus asked, urging him to look beneath the surface of the miracle. Peter squirmed and probably contorted his face, trying to guess the answer to Jesus' question. Again Jesus urges him, "Remember, it was My Father in Heaven who revealed to you who I really am (Matthew 16:17). How did He reveal that insight to you?" Jesus knew Peter had the ability to hear the Holy Spirit and gain revelation. He was trying to get him to see and hear with the eyes and ears of his spirit, not just be logical and focus on the external.

We are all trained to use our natural senses of touch, smell, hearing, taste and seeing. But God has given us more than just our natural senses. He is trying to get us trained to use our "feelings", our spiritual "intuition", our spiritual sight and hearing.

I remember once sitting at home studying when Anne, my first wife, was still alive. A lady had called to see her to collect something, so Anne had invited her into the house for a few minutes and introduced me to her. I looked up from my books, greeted her and asked a simple question, "How are you?", to which she replied, like everyone usually does, "I'm fine, thank you." Suddenly, my emotions changed in a split second. All of a sudden I felt hurt, fear, confusion and I began to well up with tears. I looked up and replied to this lady, "Then why do I feel like ..." and shared all the feelings my heart was experiencing and the thoughts that were running through my head. This dear lady immediately burst into tears in shock and told us that everything I had described, she was feeling deep inside! Anne and I had the pleasure of leading that lady in a prayer of salvation. The Holy Spirit had brought her to us and awoken my spiritual awareness so this lady could be brought to the point of accepting Jesus as her Savior.

Peter listened to his heart and suddenly insight and revelation began to flow. He knew Jesus was the Messiah, the Son of God, but now He saw clearly and began to systematically communicate what was flowing out of His heart:

"You spoke words and the words came to pass ...

You are THE Word of God and everything You say comes to pass ...

You created all things we can see or can't see by the power of your Word ..."

"Yes, yes, yes!" Jesus began to shout for joy, just as He had done when the disciples came back from being sent out by Him, reporting that demons were cast out and everyone had been healed when they prayed for them (Matthew 10:21).

"Yes, Peter. What else can you see?" Jesus asked.

"The Word of God is as powerful today when you speak it, as it was the very day you spoke all of creation into existence by the power of your Word!"

I have no doubt that Jesus was ecstatic as one revelation after another flowed out of Peter's spirit.

"If, when *You* speak the Word today it comes to pass, then when we speak the Word of God it will come to pass for us just as it does for You. For the Word of God coming out of my mouth is as powerful as when it comes out of Gods mouth!"

Even Peter is exploding now as faith is flowing in his heart, for *"faith comes from hearing and hearing by the Word of God"* (Romans 10:17). When we speak the Word of God and our ears hear it, it drops down into our spirit and creates more faith. Then, when we speak it again, this time it is with more faith, and so on and so on. It is a divine cycle.

Jesus urges Peter one more time to open to the Spirit of revelation. "Peter, when did the miracle happen?" He asks. Peter's eyes look deeply into Jesus' trying to figure out what else there can be to say. A light comes into his eyes and he smiles: "It happened yesterday, the moment You spoke the word to the tree. It was working when we walked past it last night. We couldn't see it with our eyes because it was dark, but the miracle had already happened."

Just because we can't see the Word of God working, it doesn't mean it isn't. It works the moment we believe in it and speak it out. Peter continued, "It's no good just believing the Word, we have to speak it out to release its power into our circumstances! And when we speak the Word of God into a situation, it enters the unseen realm and breaks the power at its source." Peter had remembered John the Baptist's preaching:

"And even now the axe is laid to the root of the trees. Therefore every tree which does not bear good fruit is cut down and thrown into the fire." (Luke 3:9)

He knew Jesus was the Word of God, but now he realized the axe John was referring to was also the Word of God. The axe, when laid to the root of the problem by being spoken, could cut out the roots of the problem and eventually the tree (the problem) would fall and die.

I believe Peter began to shake in awe of this revelation, just as I do from time to time when the Holy Spirit explodes within me some insight that has the power to turn my world upside down.

Grabbing and holding Peter's face in His hands, Jesus declared,

"Yes, and in just a few hours, Peter, I will hang upon a tree, lifted up between Heaven and Earth, just like this fig tree stands between Bethany and Jerusalem. And it will be on a hill, just like this hill, that my blood will be poured out as a ransom for all of man's sin, sicknesses, diseases, failures and hurts from the first sin of Adam and Eve to the very last sin that mankind ever commits. All of God's wrath and anger towards sin will be unleashed upon Me instead of you. The penalty that should be paid for every sin and all the consequences of sin will be paid for in full by the giving of my life and the shedding of my blood, because you can't redeem yourself. My blood will run down the tree into the ground and will flow all the way back 4,000 years to the tree where Adam sinned in the Garden of Eden. My perfect blood will destroy the roots of that tree of the knowledge of sin and death, lay an axe at its roots, that no longer will its power have dominion over anyone. My blood will redeem from the curse of sin and death every person who has ever lived and my blessing will flow in their lives instead of the curse. Then, anyone who comes to this cross and tree at Calvary, and accepts by faith that I am the perfect Lamb of God who takes away the sin of the world, will find forgiveness for their sins and I will remove the consciousness of sin from their hearts and break the power of the curse of sin operating in their lives."

The disciples don't fully understand all Jesus is saying to them, but they are aware of the magnitude of what He is describing. They are aware something monumental is about to happen which will change everything they have ever known and everyone who has ever lived. He is about to usher in a new day, a new order, a new beginning as miraculous as Genesis 1:1 and they know they have a major part to play in it.

Speak to your mountain,
or your mountain will speak to you

While the disciples are still trying to absorb all Jesus is saying to them He continues to challenge the walls of limitation in their mindsets by saying,

*"Have **faith** in God. For assuredly, I say to you, whoever **says** to **this** mountain, 'Be removed and be cast into the sea,' and does not doubt in his heart, but believes that those things he **says** will be done, he will have whatever he says. Therefore I say to you, whatever things you ask when you pray, **believe** that you receive them, and you will have them."* (Mark 11:22-24)

Can you imagine what must have been going through the minds of the disciples at this moment? The Mount of Olives is a mountain that has been in its geographical location since God spoke creation into existence. It's mentioned in Scripture as far back as the days of king David who wept upon it (2 Samuel 15:30). Jerusalem without the Mount of Olives is unthinkable. It's impossible to remove! Yet, Jesus is saying it can be removed just by *their* prayers, faith and words!

Can it be possible for man to remove a mountain by something as seemingly insignificant as mere words? Don't let God catch you thinking like that! He knows words are very powerful. He spoke creation into being by the power of His Word and holds it in its place by the same "word power" (Hebrews 1:3).

Joshua led the people of Israel around Jericho silently six times, but on the seventh time all Israel shouted a shout of praise, blew their trumpets and the molecular structure within those huge walls suddenly came apart. The walls that were so wide three chariots could race side by side around the top, disintegrated in front of Israel's eyes. When it happened, everyone who watched the miracle must have thought, "That is impossible!" Yet, they had seen it happen with their own eyes.

Jesus spoke to Lazarus who had been dead for four days and

buried deep inside a grave and he came back to life, walking out of the tomb still bound by the embalming clothes. Those who stood there that day watching Lazarus emerge must have been saying under their breath, "That's not possible!" Yet, once again, they saw it with their own eyes.

Moses was told by God to simply speak to a rock and water would pour out of it. He did and it did! That's impossible (Exodus 17:6)!

Thousands of people were dying in the camp from being bitten by a plague of poisonous snakes when God told Moses to erect a bronze snake on a pole in the middle of the camp. The Lord said if the people just looked upon the snake they would not die. The plague stopped and those bitten by the snakes did not die (Numbers 21:8). That is impossible!

Moses parted the Red Sea by holding out a rod made of wood over the water and billions of gallons of water started flowing in the opposite direction, mounting up as two walls of water, leaving dry land in between for Israel to cross over (Exodus 14:16)! "Hello?" That's impossible!

Joshua spoke to the sun and it stood still throughout the day until his battle was finished (Joshua 10:12). My dear friend, that has to be one of the all time, greatest supernatural events in history, yet it is impossible!

But isn't that the theme of the entire Bible? The God who can do all things man thinks are impossible, is raising up a generation of Christians who believe not only that He can do supernatural things, but by faith in His Word, so can we, His children. Isn't that what inspires us to take leaps of faith, because His Word causes us to see that nothing is impossible to those who believe?

"So Jesus said to them, 'For assuredly, I say to you, if you have

faith *as a mustard seed, you will **say** to this **mountain**, "Move from here to there," and it will move; and nothing will be impossible for you.'"* (Matthew 17:20)

Stinking thinking!

Mountains and obstacles are not just physical. In fact, I personally think the greatest mountains and obstacles to overcome are within each person. Your greatest obstacle is the "mountain" that holds your ears apart! It's our internal mountains and obstacles that create the mindset that something is impossible. Then we look upon the external mountain, obstacle or situation and say to ourselves, "It's impossible, it can't change!"

I call these mindsets our *stinking thinking*. They stand between where we are and where we desire to be, telling us that it is impossible for us (or the situation) to change for the better. The Mount of Olives stood between Bethany, Bethphage and Jerusalem and was, in just the same way, representing a mindset to those disciples that something so great was impossible to move. But Jesus was challenging the very core belief system of every man, women and child on the planet. When something is *impossible* in our eyes it begins to master us, control us, keeping us firmly rooted where we are. Jesus is challenging us to rise above the thought patterns and belief systems of this world. He is asking us to think like God who sees nothing as impossible. Everything is possible to those who believe!

"But Jesus looked at them and said to them, 'With men this is impossible, but with God all things are possible.'" (Matthew 19:26)

Jesus was teaching them the greatest lesson of their lives: how to turn everything around in life by the power of His Word coming out of their mouths. They knew God had created everything in the beginning by His Word. They saw Jesus do it so many times when people needed miracles. But Jesus was asking them to make the greatest leap of faith and begin a reformation by believing the Lord was now going to raise up a "new creation" of sons and daughters who would rule, reign and restore in life through the power of His Word spoken out of their mouths. This was the reason Jesus took three of His last four days to march the disciples back and forth over this mountain. So that on the third day they "got" it.

Right now you may be in a place of poverty, brokenness, loneliness, grief or division, yet you long to be in a place of prosperity, wholeness, joy, peace and unity. The problem is, you just can't see any way to get there from where you are right now. That, my friend, is the reason why the Lord has led me to write this book. It is to help all who read it understand that this was the very lesson Jesus spent His last days getting His disciples to understand.

He was teaching them that He was not just going to die to save mankind from their sin, so all who believed in Him could go to Heaven. It would mean that, but His death and resurrection would mean so much more! He was preparing them to understand that the work He would do on the cross of Calvary and in the tomb would ultimately lead to a miracle that would change the very nature of every person who truly believed in Christ. It would lead to Christ, through His Holy Spirit, transferring His life and power into the hearts of His followers, so that they would be immediately transferred from one kingdom to another. He would give them a new heart, a new spirit, and empower them to overcome all the works of Satan that tried to resist them. God was about to invest His heavenly power into earthly vessels, empowering them to do the very same works that Christ had been doing before their eyes. What He could do now, through the Holy Spirit's anointing, they would do also.

"But you are a chosen generation, a royal priesthood, a holy nation, His own special people, that you may proclaim the praises of Him who called you out of darkness into His marvelous light; who once were not a people but are now the people of God" (1 Peter 2:9-10)

"Most assuredly, I say to you, he who believes in Me, the works that I do he will do also; and greater works than these he will do, because I go to My Father. And whatever you ask in My name, that I will do, that the Father may be glorified in the Son. If you ask anything in My name, I will do it." (John 14:12-14)

"You are of God, little children, and have overcome them, because He who is in you is greater than he who is in the world." (1 John 4:4)

"'No weapon formed against you shall prosper, And every tongue which rises against you in judgment you shall condemn. This is the heritage of the servants of the Lord, and their righteousness is from Me,' says the LORD." (Isaiah 54:17)

"'And these signs will follow those who believe: In My name they will cast out demons; they will speak with new tongues; they will take up serpents; and if they drink anything deadly, it will by no means hurt them; they will lay hands on the sick, and they will recover.' So then, after the Lord had spoken to them, He was received up into heaven, and sat down at the right hand of God. And they went out and preached everywhere, the Lord working with them and confirming the word through the accompanying signs." (Mark 16:17-20)

The offer of abundant life

Jesus, through His death and resurrection, was opening a door that had been closed to man for 4,000 years, since Adam sinned in the garden (Genesis 3:24). Jesus was inviting the disciples and us, His Church, to step out of the kingdom of limitation and survival, and step through a door called faith into a new dimension of *"abundant life"* (John 10:10).

God did not send Jesus, His Son, into this world to suffer the ridicule and pain of death on a cross just so those who believed in Him would live a pretty "normal" life, being morally upright, good people. Yes, we are to live a life that is morally pure. We are to be gracious, kind, honoring and loving in this messed up world. But we're not called to live a life void of His *power*. The disciples walked in limited power while Jesus lived on earth. But after His death and resurrection, these very same disciples who only operated in supernatural power when He laid hands upon them and commissioned them to go out and preach in the villages, were now preaching the Gospel of Christ with signs following them. They were doing what He had been doing.

Peter so moved in power that as he walked by, people who were sick were healed even as his shadow passed over them. The early Church in the book of Acts followed in the same manner. Paul says of the Church in Galatia,

*"Therefore He who supplies the Spirit to you and works **miracles** among you, does He do it by the works of the law, or by the **hearing of faith**?"* (Galatians 3:5)

The evidence of the miraculous was a normal part of daily life for the disciples and the early Church. Scripture mentions that even the deacons, Stephen and Phillip, flowed in the supernatural power of the Holy Spirit. God desires it to be just the same for us who believe today. His power has not diminished in 2000 years, nor has His will changed.

"For I am the LORD, I do not change" (Malachi 3:6)

"Not a word failed of any good thing which the Lord had spoken to the house of Israel. All came to pass." (Joshua 21:45)

*"Having been born again, not of corruptible seed but incorruptible, through the **word** of God which lives and **abides forever,** because 'All flesh is as grass, and all the glory of man as the flower of the grass. The grass withers, and its flower falls away, but the **word of the LORD endures forever.**' Now this is the **word** which by the gospel was preached to you."* (1 Peter 1:23-25)

God's Word *is* His will. If you want to know the will of God about anything, then look into His Word and you will find it. His Word is unchanging, therefore His mind is also unchanging. If He has declared it, then He will perform it! Over and over again the Word confirms this. Look at these scriptures:

*"Blessed be the LORD, who has given rest to His people Israel, according to all that He promised. There has **not failed one word of all His good promise,** which He promised [spoke] through His servant Moses."* (1 Kings 8:56)

*"My covenant I will not break, **Nor alter the word** that has gone [been spoken] out of My lips."* (Psalm 89:34)

*"Forever, O LORD, Your **word is settled** in heaven. Your faithfulness [God's faithfulness to His Word] endures to **all** generations [that means today's generation]."* (Psalm 119:89-90)

*"So shall My **word** be that goes forth [is spoken] from My mouth;*

it shall not return to Me void, but it shall accomplish what I please, and it shall prosper in the thing for which I sent it." (Isaiah 55:11) (Notice there is no time limit mentioned here)

*"'For I am the LORD. I **speak**, and the **word** which I **speak will** [without doubt] come to pass; it will no more be postponed; for in your days, O rebellious house, I will **say** the **word** and **perform** it,' says the Lord GOD."* (Ezekiel 12:25)

Do you notice the pattern that is revealed in these scriptures? We see the same pattern in many other scriptures about God's Word:

- He speaks His Word.

- He fulfils His Word.

- His Word is faithful.

- His Word is unchanging, settled.

- His Word is for all generations. That means everyone, everywhere at anytime. That means YOU – not just people you think must be special so that the Lord uses them. Miracles are happening in every nation of the world right now through the hands of a few evangelists and preachers. It's time to wake up God's sleeping giant, His Church! It's time for the whole body of Christ to walk in His power and provision. That's what He died for, not just to save us and give us a home in Heaven when we get there!

The glory of the latter house

Imagine if we could see every believer in the body of Christ flowing in their God-given authority and power, seeing miracles on a daily basis even greater than the early Church. Then, surely, we would see the Church having an even greater effect in the earth in our generation than the early Church did in theirs! Because,

*" 'The glory of this **latter temple** shall be **greater than the former,** ' says the Lord of hosts. 'And in this place I will give **peace,** ' says the LORD of hosts. "* (Haggai 2:9)

The book of Acts and all the Holy Spirit did with the early Church is the "former house". The glory of God being revealed now, and yet to be revealed in our generation, is the glory of the "latter house". The end of God's work is always greater than its beginning.

I prophesy to you that this is exactly what Jesus was trying to communicate to His disciples on the Mount of Olives those three final days before He went to the cross. He was asking them to make a leap of faith, to tear down, uproot, overthrow and cast out all their preconceptions of who He was and what He could do, and realize that there was no limit to God's power in them and to what He could do through them. In the next seven weeks He would destroy their comfort zones, mess with their theology, break their traditions and laws, sweep aside their preconceived ideas, make them face every fear they had within them, and take them on a journey of self-discovery to remove their "unfinished business". They were not ready to receive all He needed to give to them, so their old "wineskins" were about to be removed and they would never be the same again! This is exactly the same thing He is trying to do in your life today.

CHAPTER 14

YOUR FINEST HOUR ~ DAY 3, PART 2

The mountain of doubt

Jesus was asking His disciples to step through the door of faith, leave an existence of mediocrity and enter into a life of significance. The cry for significance is the cry of every heart. It is the fear of insignificance that creates the hostile world we live in. It can be the reason for war. It is at the root of breakdowns in relationships. It drives a generation to try to gain it through education, status, titles or logo's on the clothes they wear and the possessions they have. It fuels the drive to maintain certain relationships due to the erroneous belief that who we know will give us the significance we desire. When those relationships end, our deep rooted sense of insignificance is exposed in a moment and thoughts of self-rejection, guilt, anger, fear – even depression, suicide and murder – can flood in. This is when, tragically, we often curse ourselves with the words, "I will *never, ever* let this happen again …"

Insignificance can attack a person during the grieving process of the death of a loved one, at the end of a marriage, when our children have grown up, have moved on in life and no longer "need" us. It can happen even when we leave a job we've been in for many years.

The fear of insignificance has driven women to manipulate situations so they can become pregnant, because they believe being a mother will give them the significance they desire.

The fear of insignificance has played a major part in the breakdown of families in our generation. It has caused parents to give their children everything they want, even if it is unreasonable to do so and puts the parents into debt. Parents do things like this because they want their child to appreciate them. They fail to bring discipline and correction into the life of their child, allowing him/her to run riot, all because the parent has a "need" to be needed and accepted by the child they are raising. They have failed to realize that firm, loving discipline is what every child looks for from birth. A child needs stability and guidelines to feel safe. By not giving a child an environment of good, balanced discipline, a parent actually communicates that they do not care about the child's welfare.

A child is looking for significance in the eyes of their parents. When that need goes unmet the child can grow up with anger in their heart that will eventually explode into the open in some destructive way. Why? Because they have not learned what respect means. A lack of discipline communicates to a child that they are not respected or valued – and if a child is not valued, they in turn can grow up not ascribing value or respect to those around them, such as those in authority or even their siblings. Remember, you can't give what you have not first received.

For a child to grow up with an inward knowledge that they are significant and can do something significant with their life, they must first receive it from someone else, such as a parent. If a parent struggles with a deep sense of insignificance, how can they pass a sense of significance onto their child? They can't! So that person has to find someone who can break their inner belief system of insignificance and release within them a conviction and knowledge of their intrinsic value and significance.

"We love Him because He first loved us." (1 John 4:19)

Someone's perfectly consistent love towards us communicates that we are of worth and significance to them. But this is only half the truth. We now have to learn to value, respect and love ourselves to get the best out of our life. Someone can love and respect us, but if we don't have the revelation of how significant we are, then the moment they stop showing it to us for some reason, we fall apart and insignificance floods our soul. When we do carry the awareness of our significance, then our emotional state is stable because it is not dependent upon someone else meeting our needs to make us feel good about ourselves or our life.

I believe Jesus was teaching His disciples, and wants to teach us today, that the "mountain" of insignificance can and has to be removed from our heart for us to make the shift from our "Bethany" to His "Jerusalem".

A faulty Gospel

Over the centuries preachers have preached a message they have called the Gospel of Jesus Christ, but which has left many believing that God does not really value or *like* people. Their message has been one of "turn or burn", projecting the image of an angry God who condemns every person who is not perfect. Their message has been about God striking people down in judgment and wrath because they made mistakes and that their destiny is now a terrible Hell where they will be tortured in an everlasting fire. They have preached that people are "unacceptable" because they wear certain clothes, smoke or drink alcohol. In fact, they preach as if God Himself would fall from His throne with convulsions if they ever went to a cinema on a Sunday, read any version of the Bible other than the Authorized Version, enjoyed country and western music or had a good sexual relationship with their spouse!

Through their preaching they have made some believers feel guilty because they cannot attend every meeting in the church calendar, calling them "uncommitted" to the Lord, when the issue isn't their commitment, just simply the fact that they don't attend church meetings five nights per week! (How can we ever reach the world with His great Gospel of grace if we are in church meetings all week?) Notice, their gospel is all about what we're *not* supposed to do.

I know such people mean well, but the communication of such a poor reflection of the Gospel has left a legacy of wrong doctrine and the erroneous belief that God is unhappy with us unless we are perfectly perfect! Of course, perfection is impossible to attain both for ourselves and the preacher who preaches that message! It is no less than a re-preaching of the Old Testament Law in a New Testament environment. It didn't work then and it won't work now. That's why the Gospel of Jesus is called the "Gospel of grace" (Acts 20:24; Galatians 1:6)

I grew up in a Methodist church and I have many wonderful memories of the years my family raised me in that environment. I know they taught me good things and I am thankful for that. But I also can remember being told that God would not answer my prayer for the healing of my cough, or about my need for a job. Oh no, I was told, that was too trivial a matter for God to worry about. After all, He had the whole world to care about. His mind was on the starving multitudes in far off places.

Without realizing it, these people were showing me their own deep rooted belief system that had been reproduced in them by the church generation before them. It said that God did not care for them, the individual, He only really cared for "others". Over the years this lie had persuaded them to believe they were really quite insignificant to God. But because they thought this lie was the truth, they preached it and perpetuated it.

But something happened in me the day I was born again that transformed my belief system and made me realize I am incredibly valuable to God. I would like to share this simple thing with you now. I believe the Holy Spirit is right there with you, at this moment, touching your heart to heal you and to begin the work that will deliver you from all the lies of insignificance that have made you feel of no importance to God, yourself and those around you. If you're ready to begin this journey with the Holy Spirit, then just pray to Him right now and tell Him you are ready. Give Him your permission to break you free from the lies of insignificance.

*"For God so **loved** the world that He **gave** His **only** begotten Son, that whoever believes in Him should not perish but have everlasting life. For God did **not** send His Son into the world to **condemn** the world, but that the world through Him might be **saved.**"* (John 3:16-17)

These were the very first Bible verses given to me to read when I gave my life to Christ. As I read them over and over again I burst into tears. I had been such a failure in my own eyes and felt so bad about the things I had done wrong, even though I had not actually done much wrong in life! I was under conviction of my sin. But then that wonderful day happened in my life when I confessed to God I was a sinner and needed His help. Right there on my living room floor I experienced the greatest flow of forgiveness and love I could ever experience. It cleansed me from the inside out. As I read those verses from John's Gospel my heart was literally crying as the Holy Spirit opened my eyes to see that this awesome God who created everything just by His words, who was totally Holy, unreachable because He was so Holy, who could blink His eye and wipe away mountains, who could snap His fingers and every star would vaporize, had actually given Jesus, His only Son, to go to the cross in *my* place. And, He had done it all because He loved ME! Not just everyone else. I realized in a moment that I had to be incredibly valuable to God for four reasons:

1. He paid for me with Someone who was perfect and priceless. No one would ever pay such a high price for something that was fake or worthless to them. People only pay the highest of prices for a masterpiece, something that is of immense value to them. People will go to extraordinary lengths to acquire a precious work of art, even if others cannot see what they see in it.

2. He sent Jesus into the world. In other words, He sent Jesus to find me because I was lost, even though I didn't even know I was lost. I wasn't even seeking Him, yet He was seeking me. The initiative was on His side. I was a lamb who had strayed and the Good Shepherd had left what He was doing to come and find me. Why? Because He loved me and could hear me in the distance crying out to be significant, to someone.

3. He saved Me. In order to save me He had to forgive me and wipe the slate clean of all my failures and sin. And He did. I didn't have to earn it, I just had to ask Him to do it.

4. He didn't come to condemn me. The word "condemn" in the original Greek of the New Testament means "to try (as in a court of law), punish or distinguish" (Strong's 2919). Jesus didn't come to put me on trial for my failures. If He had, I would have been found guilty. But instead He went to the cross and declared me "not guilty!" He didn't come to punish me, He came to heal and reconcile me to Himself, to restore to me everything I had lost because of the destructive consequences of sin. He didn't extinguish the flame of my life, but put His spirit within me and ignited me with His kind of life that can never go out! Instead of being extinguished He gave me a distinction! Top marks instead of failure! He isn't trying to destroy lives, but give completely new ones to those who turn to Him for help. Our message and communication of His Gospel must be the same.

"But God demonstrates His own love toward us, in that while we were still sinners, Christ died for us." (Romans 5:8)

He has always loved us. Love isn't demonstrated by being judgmental, angry or accusative to someone. Love is cherishing, kind, patient, forbearing, always thinking and communicating the best of someone. Love is trusting, not controlling.

"Eye has not seen, nor ear heard, nor have entered into the heart of man the things which God has prepared for those who love Him." (1 Corinthians 2:9)

Because He loves you, He has already planned wonderful things for you for the rest of your life that are so magnificent they are beyond your wildest dreams.

"For in Christ Jesus neither circumcision nor un-circumcision avails anything, but faith working through love." (Galatians 5:6)

The more we get a revelation of how much God loves us, the greater force of faith we have and it is faith that overcomes all things.

"That Christ may dwell in your hearts through faith; that you, being rooted and grounded in love, may be able to comprehend with all the saints what is the width and length and depth and height to know the love of Christ which passes knowledge; that you may be filled with all the fullness of God." (Ephesians 3:17-19)

The greater the depth of our revelation of His love for us, the greater our revelation of who we are in Christ, who He is within us and what He can do through us.

"For God has not given us a spirit of fear, but of power and of love and of a sound mind." (2 Timothy 1:7)

So if God didn't give us a spirit of fear, where did we get it from? Look at this next verse:

"There is no fear in love; but perfect love casts out fear, because fear involves torment. But he who fears has not been made perfect in love. We love Him because He first loved us." (1 John 4:18-19)

Fear exists in our life only because we have an absence of His love. His love in our heart protects us from fear. But this verse says that fear exists because it involves torment. Let me remind you what we discovered earlier: *fear thrives on guilt.* If we experience fear, it is because we are open to feelings of guilt! Some people feel guilty because they really have done something wrong. Others *have* a permanent guilty conscience, even though they haven't done anything wrong.

If we feel guilty, we fear what people will say or do if they discover what we did, or think we did, that was wrong. The moment it looks to us like our sin will be found out, fear grips our heart and we lose our peace. But what *really* happened deep down in our heart is that we lost sight and let go of the truth that God loves us unconditionally. He loves you and me at all times! He loves even those who reject what He did for them at the cross of Calvary and would sooner spend eternity in Hell rather than accept His forgiveness. He *is* love. He doesn't *have* love, because that implies there may times when He doesn't feel or have love. He *is* love. It's who He is, permanently.

Resisting the devil with God's Word

During times and seasons when we get attacked by the spirit of fear, we must learn to,

"Resist the devil [fear] *and he will flee from you."* (James 4:7)

How do we resist him? The same way Jesus resisted him! We speak the Word of God to him and to the situations he instigates that contradict the will and Word of God.

"And the devil said to Him, 'If You are the Son of God, command this stone to become bread.'

> *But Jesus answered him, saying, 'It is written, "Man shall not live by bread alone, but by every word of God."'*

> *Then the devil, taking Him up on a high mountain, showed Him all the kingdoms of the world in a moment of time. And the devil said to Him, 'All this authority I will give You, and their glory; for this has been delivered to me, and I give it to whomever I wish. Therefore, if You will worship before me, all will be Yours.'*

> *And Jesus answered and said to him, 'Get behind Me, Satan!* **For it is written,** *"You shall worship the Lord your God, and Him only you shall serve."'*

> *Then he brought Him to Jerusalem, set Him on the pinnacle of the temple, and said to Him, 'If You are the Son of God, throw Yourself down from here.* **For it is written:**

> *"He shall give His angels charge over you,*
> *to keep you,"*
> *and,*
> *"in their hands they shall bear you up, lest you dash your foot against a stone."'*

> *And Jesus answered and said to him, 'It has been said, "You shall not tempt the LORD your God."'"* (Luke 4:3-12)

When Satan desired to tempt Jesus to sin he visited Him during a vulnerable moment when Jesus was weak from fasting. He was hungry. Satan always comes to attack the people of God when we are vulnerable. He never comes when we are strong and full of faith and confidence because he knows we would be too powerful for him to defeat. So, he comes at our weak moments.

Satan came to deceive Jesus into trying to fulfill God's will Himself, without doing it God's way or in His timing. Notice he attempted to make Jesus believe that if He did things Satan's way he would still be fulfilling God's will for His life. That's real temptation. "Don't do it via the cross and sacrifice your life," Satan suggests. "I'll give everything to you. All you have to do is worship me."

Temptation is only temptation if it tempts us! When I am on a diet to lose some weight, I know I have to focus on eating certain things and be careful to stay disciplined until I reach my target weight. An offer of something I don't like to eat will not tempt me to break the diet. What tempts me during that diet is when someone offers to buy me the most scrumptious cake or a Starbucks coffee! It's a temptation because something inside tells me I will feel so much better if I take what is on offer.

Satan never wastes his time trying to tempt us out of God's will for our life with something that will not lure us. He was trying to persuade Jesus that He could fulfill His natural hunger by turning stones into bread, using His God-given power to meet His own needs. This would never have been a temptation if Jesus was not hungry or didn't have the power to do it!

WOW! Jesus had the power to literally turn stones into bread. Satan was trying to get Jesus to break His fast early, when God had told Jesus to fast for 40 days and 40 nights. Satan knew that Jesus had to walk perfectly before God and man to fulfill the work

God had given Him to do. So it was essential He stayed faithful to God's word. Jesus needed to remain obedient and stay under God's authority to receive the power and authority to overcome the works of the devil.

When Jesus heard Satan's words of temptation He took Gods written Word and spoke it back at him. Each time Satan came at Jesus with a new temptation Jesus did the same thing: He spoke the Word of God back to Satan and eventually Satan departed from him. Jesus was showing us that this is the way to defeat the devil every time he comes to tempt you or attack you. You speak the Word of God to him or to the situation that has become like a mountain to you and is preventing you from breaking free and stepping into a new level of victory and freedom.

Why use the Word? Why does the devil back off from us when we do this? Because he is subject to God's Word and God's Word spoken out of our mouth is no different than when it's spoken out of Gods mouth! Whether it comes out of His mouth or ours it is still the Word of God and the devil and all of creation is subject to the Word of God. Everything God created He created with His spoken Word. Everything broken and out of line with His Word will be healed and brought back into line by the same Word. All of creation will come into line with His spoken Word when someone, whose heart is fully persuaded and full of faith that God's Word has power over all the works of the devil, speaks it out at the devil or the mountains they face in life.

Gods written Word covers every situation and circumstance in life, so we can always find scriptures that answer our need or situation and speak them out in faith. The more we speak them out, the more we will hear them and *"faith comes by hearing and hearing by the Word of God"* (Romans 10:17). The more we hear the Word of God the more faith grows in our heart, until the faith in our heart is greater than the obstacle or mountain we face. *Then,* we will speak to our mountain and it will move! It is not *you or me* doing the work, but Christ, the Word of God, doing it through us.

"It is written"

Psalm 45:1 says,

*"My **tongue** is the pen of a ready writer."*

Notice what the Psalmist says. He describes his tongue as a pen. A pen is used to write or inscribe words on paper or, in the days of the psalmist, on "tablets" of stone or paper. But on what does a tongue inscribe and engrave? The answer is our own heart! We speak words over and over until those words are etched into our heart, which is why the Bible says,

*"Keep your **heart** with all diligence, for out of it spring the issues of life. Put away from you a deceitful **mouth**, and put perverse lips far from you."* (Proverbs 4:23-24)

Our words matter. They are powerful. Our words impact us before they impact anyone else and have more impact on us than upon anyone else. The word "issues" used in this verse means "the boundaries or source" of our life. In other words, our own words are the source of the life we live. Our world, our life and our days are ordered and limited by our own mouths. This means we can put limitations on our life or remove them by the very words that proceed from our mouth. If we don't like the kind of life we are experiencing, then we need to look at what is flowing out of our mouth on a daily basis. It may be that we are not overcoming our mountain of debt, sickness, temptation or relationship problems because our mouth is keeping us limited in life and bound to our past experience.

The Lord showed me a long time ago that I could only receive in life what my words and mouth said I could have. In other words, we won't have any more than that which our mouth confesses! We put limits on our life or remove them by what we speak about our life. Our words are writing upon our hearts every day and our hearts (spirits) are like a sponge. They believe whatever we speak to them! Our heart doesn't have its own opinions. We tell our heart what to believe and it believes what we say. It is so imperative to understand this process. I really want you to grasp this truth with all of your heart. Our future is not determined by our past. It is determined by what we believe and say. It has nothing to do with how our mother or father treated us. It has nothing to do with how the government failed us or let us down when we needed help. It has nothing to do with our level of education, the color of our skin or the country we live in. But it has everything to do with what we have said throughout our life, for our heart believes what we say. It is our servant and will do whatever we say to it. This is why the Lord spoke to Joshua the way He did as he stood on the borders of Canaan, pondering how to lead Israel into the promises of God for their lives:

*"**This Book of the Law** shall not depart from your **mouth**, but you shall **meditate** in it day and night, that you may observe to do according to all that is written in it. For then you will make your way prosperous, and then you will have good success."* (Joshua 1:8)

The Lord showed Joshua as he stood facing the land of Canaan with its mountains, its great walled cities and its giants that needed to be overcome in order to establish Israel in the place God intended them to be, that his victories over his enemies would be determined by his obedience in meditating upon God's Word day and night.

The psalmist and king Solomon both repeated this thought in their writings:

*"But his delight is in the **law of the L*ord*,** and in His law he **meditates** day and night. He shall be like a tree planted by the rivers of water, that brings forth its fruit in its season, whose leaf also shall not wither; **and whatever he does shall prosper.**"* (Psalm 1:2-3)

*"My son, keep my **words**, and treasure my **commands** within you. Keep my commands and live, and my **law** as the apple of your eye. Bind them on your fingers; **write them on the tablet of your heart.**"* (Proverbs 7:1-3)

Biblical meditation is not the same as the meditation taught by those who teach Yoga. Yoga classes teach people to empty their mind of all stressful and harmful thoughts so that they can come to a place of peace. Biblical meditation is the opposite. It teaches us to fill our minds constantly with God's Word by reading it and confessing it until we have memorized it. God promises that if we meditate upon His Word constantly, then those words will be written, etched upon our hearts, creating faith within us. Then our faith level will grow and grow until God's Word comes automatically out of our mouths to create new boundaries and a new life experience for us. Prosperity, health, healings, victory, deliverance, and answered prayers will be the byproduct of what we believe and confess.

His Word is His Word

Jesus is called the Word of God (John 1:1,14). He is the Word! All that Jesus is and the quality of life that He now has is free for all who believe in Him by believing on His Word. He and His Word are the same!

*"If you abide in My **word**, you are My disciples indeed."* (John 8:31)

*"If you abide in Me, and My **words** abide in you, you will ask what you desire, and it shall be done for you."* (John 15:7)

Have you ever watched other Christians living in fruitfulness and victory in an area of life where you just can't seem to get the victory? Did you wonder why God had blessed them more than you? Did you feel a sense of failure or rejection as if the Lord just wasn't listening to the cries of your heart? Yet, you know that the Bible says,

*"Then Peter opened his mouth, and said, 'Of a truth I perceive that **God is no respecter of persons.**'"* (Acts 10:34)

God has no favorites! *All* of His children are favored with the same measure of favor, including you and me. Could it just be that you suffer in some areas of life with low self esteem or *stinking thinking*, therefore you struggle to believe that God's Word will work for you the same as it does for others? Could it be that you have said, "I've tried confessing His Word, but it didn't work for me"? When the truth is, you did it for a short time, but when a tough time came along you reverted back to your old ways of thinking, speaking and acting, so you didn't see the breakthrough?

God's Word does not work better for one person than another, or in one country better than another. God's Word works for everyone who believes in Him and His Word. But it is not a "quick fix" to our situation. Living in the fullness of His promises is not the result of simply confessing His Word today and expecting everything to land in our lap tomorrow. The lifestyle He promises in His Word is the result of two things working in our life: *relationship* and *meditation*!

How would we feel if our children or friends only visited us to get what was in our larder or bank balance, but didn't really love us or have time for us as a person? What any good parent would do is withhold what they have from their children until they learn to love the giver more than the gifts we give them. God is a Father and desires His children to know Him and have a loving relationship with Him. We cannot have an attitude that takes for granted His name or His Word and grabs what He gives to lavish it on ourselves with no sense of gratitude. Prosperity, peace, joy, victory and every other thing He promises are byproducts of us abiding in Him and Him living His life in and through us.

Jesus said,

"I am the vine, you are the branches. He who abides in Me, and I in him, bears much fruit; for without Me you can do nothing. If anyone does not abide in Me, he is cast out as a branch and is withered; and they gather them and throw them into the fire, and they are burned. If you abide in Me, and My words abide in you, you will ask what you desire, and it shall be done for you. By this My Father is glorified, that you bear much fruit; so you will be My disciples." (John 15:5-8)

John's Gospel shows the connection between our relationship with Jesus as we abide in Him and meditating upon His Words. Together they produce the fruitful lifestyle we long for. Every time you read the Word of God, speak it out in faith and your tongue will write the words you spoke upon the tablet of your heart, deep within you. The more you speak them, the more they will be reinforced and engraved onto your heart. The more His Word is stored within you, the stronger you will become because His Word becomes a fortress within you. The more you meditate upon the Word of God, the more you will become full of it and when you keep on filling your heart then eventually it will begin to overflow the Word of God. As Jesus said,

"A good man out of the good treasure of his heart brings forth

good; and an evil man out of the evil treasure of his heart brings forth evil. For out of the abundance of the heart his mouth speaks. " (Luke 6:45)

Jesus says that whatever we are full of flows out of our mouth. What comes out of your mouth? Words! Words that reflect what you are full of. If you wish to know what you are full of, then listen to the things you say.

CHAPTER 15

A CRY FOR REAL COMMUNION

"And whenever you stand praying, if you have anything against anyone, forgive him, that your Father in heaven may also forgive you your trespasses. But, if you do not forgive, neither will your Father in heaven forgive your trespasses."
(Mark 11:25-26)

In the chapters of this book I have tried to show that man has lost his completeness (peace) through the destructive consequences of sin. Man lost true freedom and ever since has revealed his inability to break free from the slavery of a sinful life. Outside of Christ we are lost in life. We have lost our identity, our security and our significance, so we try to "cover" ourselves with that which we believe will make us "acceptable" to God.

When Adam and Eve sinned, however, we see the Lord establishing a plan to rescue and restore mankind. In Genesis 3:21 the Lord *re-covered* Adam and Eve with a covering to replace the one they had lost.

Don't Kick Your Donkey, Ride It has been about this same principle and process. Bethany and Bethphage represent man's state of brokenness. Jerusalem represents our total recovery and restoration to a place of completeness and wholeness. The Mount of Olives, the tree, the donkey and the three days of walking over the Mount of Olives all speak to us of our journey of transition. They speak to us of how God has accomplished everything through the cross and the sacrifice of Jesus to pay for our sin and free us from its consequences.

On the journey of transition we learn that He has driven the thieves of self-righteousness and fear from His temple (our heart) and replaced them with His presence and love, that our heart might become a place of worship (intimacy and relationship) and prayer.

We have seen that our spiritual journey from Bethany to Jerusalem begins when we understand we are in a place of incompleteness and need God to rescue and restore us. The second step is to learning to release our faith and by speaking as Jesus did. We learn to rise up in the "God kind" of faith that Jesus spoke of in Mark 11:22 and confess His Word to our mountains of insignificance, insecurity, sickness, poverty, fear and guilt. We learn to make the confession of His Word our lifestyle, not just something we do in a stormy season in our life.

Now we have one more significant issue to examine which Jesus showed was part and parcel of this revelation. We need to learn the power and importance of unity in the family of God.

Do this in remembrance of me

Immediately the disciples had received their lesson on the Mount of Olives, Jesus led them to an upper room where He had His final meal with them. Together they sat eating what we have termed "the Last Supper". Here, in this upper room all His disciples are fully aware of the magnitude of the moment. Even if they are not fully aware of all that is about to happen, they know, from all that Jesus is saying and doing, that this is an incredibly significant time in His ministry.

"When the hour had come, He sat down, and the twelve apostles with Him. Then He said to them, 'With fervent desire I have desired to eat this Passover with you before I suffer; for I say to you, I will no longer eat of it until it is fulfilled in the kingdom of

God.' Then He took the cup, and gave thanks, and said, 'Take this and divide it among yourselves; for I say to you, I will not drink of the fruit of the vine until the kingdom of God comes.' And He took bread, gave thanks and broke it, and gave it to them, saying, 'This is My body which is given for you; do this in remembrance of Me.' Likewise He also took the cup after supper, saying, 'This cup is the new covenant in My blood, which is shed for you. But behold, the hand of My betrayer is with Me on the table. And truly the Son of Man goes as it has been determined, but woe to that man by whom He is betrayed!'" (Luke 22:14-22)

During this deep moment of fellowship as Jesus tries to comfort and at the same time strengthen this group of leaders who are not fully ready for the task that lies ahead of them, Jesus instigates a sacrament that will become central to the message of the Gospel and our life as His Church. It was the time of the Feast of Passover in Israel and everyone was gathered in Jerusalem for the occasion in obedience to God's command (Deuteronomy 16:16). Gathering together to partake of the Passover meal was not a casual event one could just take or leave. God had commanded that every family must be represented at the feast by the presence of their male heads. It was of central importance to His plans for His people. He wanted to meet with His people through this event.

The Feast of Passover celebrated and brought to Israel's remembrance the way the Lord had sent Moses to lead His people out of captivity and into Canaan, the Promised Land. In this incredible exodus from Egypt's tyrannical rule over Israel, the Lord's penultimate strike on Pharaoh was to allow the Angel of Death to "pass over" the land. Every member of an Israeli family was to gather in their home, sacrifice a spotless lamb, sprinkle its blood on the doorposts of their home and then sit around the table together to eat the lamb. At every table one chair was to remain vacant as a prophetic sign that the Messiah would one day visit them. A place was prepared for Him, their unseen guest, to partake of this feast. Each person was to dress with their clothes tucked into their belts as a sign that they were about to flee from Egypt.

As they sat eating their first ever Passover Lamb, so the Angel of Death came across the land of Egypt and every firstborn child and animal died in one night. Israel listened to the screams and cries going out across the land as they sat and humbly ate this feast on the eve of their ultimate deliverance and freedom from bondage.

So, as Jesus lifted a cup of wine before His disciples saying, *"Take this and divide it amongst yourselves"* and followed this by breaking a loaf of bread, declaring, *"This is My body which is given for you; do this is remembrance of Me,"* they were being given an illustrative sermon. That which was whole (Christ) was to be broken so that what was broken (mankind) could be made whole.

The disciples were not oblivious regarding the timing of this supper and the meaning of Jesus' words. They all knew He was the Messiah. He was sitting at the table in the place reserved and prepared for Him. They knew the wine was symbolic of the blood of the Passover lamb. They had heard John the Baptizer refer to Jesus as *"the Lamb of God who takes away the sin of the world"* (John 1:29). There, in that room, He declared the bread to be His body which was to be given for them. He tore the bread into pieces portioning it amongst them, saying, *"This is my body, given for you ..."* Then, He took the cup and announced, *"This cup is the new covenant in My blood which is shed for you."* In the silence of that upper room the imagery and symbolism were not lost on His listeners.

Jesus was revealing to all that the Old Testament Feast of Passover and all it represented was about Him, God in the flesh. It portrayed Jesus laying down His life to deliver from bondage and the curse of sin every person who would believe and trust in Him. The disciples were being asked to embrace a truth and a message that would alienate them from family, friends and their traditional teaching and beliefs. They were being invited by Jesus to preach a Gospel that revealed the Messiah was not going to come one day in the future, but indeed He was already here. He had arrived, fulfilled the meaning of the feast, and was literally laying down His life as their ransom.

Eyes were filled with tears and minds were struggling to come to terms with the magnitude of His words. Everyone was trying to cope with the heaviness of the moment. Yet here, in this most incredible atmosphere, still one found the ability to remove himself from the moment and betray the One who was about to lay down His life. Judas was about to turn his back on the One who, in an eternal act of forgiveness, would pay the price to reconcile all of mankind to the One who created them. This response of betrayal by Judas was not lost on the disciples or Paul the apostle, when He wrote to the Corinthian churches on the issue of the Lord's Supper:

"Therefore when you come together in one place, it is not to eat the Lord's Supper. For in eating, each one takes his own supper ahead of others; and one is hungry and another is drunk. What! Do you not have houses to eat and drink in? Or do you despise the church of God and shame those who have nothing? What shall I say to you? Shall I praise you in this? I do not praise you.

For I received from the Lord that which I also delivered to you: that the Lord Jesus on the same night in which He was betrayed took bread; and when He had given thanks, He broke it and said, 'Take, eat; this is My body which is broken for you; do this in remembrance of Me.' In the same manner He also took the cup after supper, saying, 'This cup is the new covenant in My blood. This do, as often as you drink it, in remembrance of Me.'

For as often as you eat this bread and drink this cup, you proclaim the Lord's death till He comes.

Therefore whoever eats this bread or drinks this cup of the Lord in an unworthy manner will be guilty of the body and blood of the Lord. But let a man examine himself, and so let him eat of the bread and drink of the cup. For he who eats and drinks in an unworthy manner eats and drinks judgment to himself, not discerning the Lord's body. For this reason many are weak and sick among you, and many sleep. For if we would judge ourselves, we would not be judged. But when we are judged, we are chastened by the Lord, that we may not be condemned with the world.

Therefore, my brethren, when you come together to eat, wait for one another. But if anyone is hungry, let him eat at home, lest you come together for judgment." (1 Corinthians 11:20-34)

The early Church never celebrated the Lord's Supper (or Communion as many call it today) as part of a service where everyone was given a morsel of bread or disk of rice paper and a sip of juice from a cup. They understood it to be a love feast where everyone would meet at a certain location, each family bringing their lunch and food with them. Everyone was encouraged to bring enough food for their family, plus a little extra for those so poor they could not provide for themselves. No quiet music was played and no priest or minister performed some ceremonial act to make it seem like a religious moment. It was a feast where the body of Christ was gathered to display their love for one another – to recognize that they were all members of the one body of Christ, the Church.

Today, many church leaders would be unable to replicate this love feast because of their doctrinal viewpoint or because of upholding denominational traditions. But in so doing they miss the central meaning and message contained within. It is all about unity, inclusion, about *re-membering* as opposed to *dis-membering* the body of Christ.

Paul instructed everyone in the churches to come together for a love feast. As they did, each was to bring food to put on the table for everyone to share and enjoy. They were not to eat their own food alone, but include other members of the church family. I remember many times watching a similar scene take place when I was pastoring a church in Wales. The more generous or wealthy would bring huge plates full of beef or chicken, while others would bring large cakes and exotic desserts. Others, who were not so well off, would bring sandwiches or some cheese or bread. We taught that *everyone* had to bring something to contribute to the whole and we would not start until the whole church family was gathered in the room. This is what I believe Paul was saying to the Corinthians.

The Corinthian Church had lost sight of the meaning of the feast. People were sitting down and eating what they had brought, not sharing it with others to create a sense of family. Some were even eating before everyone was ready and sitting down together. My mother would have reprimanded us had we done that at home! We were never allowed to begin eating a meal until all the family were seated together at the table. If someone was late or missing, one of us was sent to find them and bring them to the table. Together we ate whatever was brought to the table. It didn't matter who had placed what on the table, everyone ate of the whole contribution.

Paul the apostle teaches us in his letter that the Last Supper instituted by Jesus is a covenant meal. He teaches that we are all to partake of it when we gather together and it represents the whole body of Jesus and the sacrifice of His life and blood to establish a New Covenant with His people based upon His grace and forgiveness. Each time a person partakes of this covenant meal they are expressing the truth that they are saved and forgiven by no other virtue than the lavish grace and forgiveness of God. This meal represents our understanding that we did nothing to deserve this grace, forgiveness or salvation, it was completely and utterly the work of God based on His personal cost of Jesus' death and His benevolence towards mankind.

God's benevolence, grace and forgiveness are all received and applied into our lives as we come to Him humbly, not because of the merit of anything we have done or could ever do. We cannot earn God's favor, we can only receive it by faith in His nature, His Word and the blood of Jesus shed to redeem all of mankind from the curse of sin. That we are forgiven and brought into God's family through no merit of our own, but by the grace of God, is surely the overwhelming message of the Last Supper.

We are all asked to put on the table whatever we have to share. Through His Holy Spirit, God has gifted every one of His people with abilities, different manifestations of Himself, talents and ministries. Should we not put "on the table" our expression of thankfulness to God for His great mercy in forgiving us by sharing these gifts? Our gifts, talents, ministries and abilities should feed, nourish and nurture our brothers and sisters. What God has given us through the Holy Spirit is not just for ourselves, but given to bless those around us.

Each part of our natural bodies plays a part in our daily life, contributing to the ability and welfare of the whole body. Our arm, for instance, does not merely self-exist. A muscle is no good without a bone to attach to. Everything in the body gains life and health from the contribution of the rest. So our gifts, talents and abilities from God are to be used to bring quality of life and health to the whole body of Christ – and this means the wider body too, not just our denomination or little expression of it. Your local church is responsible to use its abilities, gifts and ministries to build up the wider body of Christ. Other churches in your town or city are to do the same for the church you attend. Today I travel the world ministering in churches of all denominations, streams and expressions. Some are large, some very small. I still go to small churches to minister on purpose. I go because I desire to help that pastor and church fulfill their God-given destiny. If I can go and share with them what I have to put on the table, then I am delighted. I don't go to "get" something from them; I go to "give" something to them that God has given me. I go to give, not take. We need to realize that it does not benefit the kingdom of God when there is one large successful church in a town. We need every church in every town growing and successfully achieving the mandate the Lord has given it. My responsibility is to help, wherever I can, build up the whole Church by using my talent, gift and ministry.

Could it be that we, the Church, have become so religious with the Lord's Table that we have lost sight of its underlying truth and message? We have turned it into a sermon and a sacrament, but we are not fulfilling its real message. We are one body with the same Master, Lord and Spirit. We preach the same Gospel of Christ and are saved by the same blood of Christ. We will all live for eternity in the same Heaven, around the same throne of God. "WE ARE FAMILY!" It's time to demonstrate our love in more than words or sermons.

"A new commandment I give to you, that you love one another; as I have loved you, that you also love one another. By this all will know that you are My disciples, if you have love for one another." (John 13:34-35)

Just a little while before Jesus went to the cross, He described the most effective evangelism technique the Church could use to reach this world with His Gospel. A technique (for want of a better word) the majority of His Church would later teach about, write about and sing eloquently about, yet rarely instigate. The early Church, seen in the first few chapters of the book of Acts, is a Church of total *unity*. They are worshipping, learning and living together, lavishly expressing what God's *agape* love looks and feels like. It was only during the time of Paul, as we can see from his letters to the Church in Rome and Corinth, that there appeared some evidence of divisions in the city wide, regional Church. His letters were not addressed to the local Baptist, Pentecostal or Independent Church in Ephesus, Corinth or Rome. Although there were gatherings and congregations of Christians meeting together in halls, houses and a variety of locations, the apostle still addressed his letters to the one Church (not churches) of that particular city or region which was read out to all when they gathered for the Lord's Table. The Church today seems terribly divided over silly issues. Maybe you feel I am wrong to say the issues are "silly", but the New Testament rightly describes divisions as "carnal" and "childish".

"And I, brethren, could not speak to you as to spiritual people but as to carnal, as to babes in Christ. I fed you with milk and not with solid food; for until now you were not able to receive it, and even now you are still not able; for you are still carnal. For where there are envy, strife, and divisions among you, are you not carnal and behaving like mere men? For when one says, 'I am of Paul,' and another, 'I am of Apollos,' are you not carnal?" (1 Corinthians 3:1-4)

Milk is for babies, not mature people, so Paul is rebuking the people for thinking and acting immaturely with an earthly mindset and attitude rather than a heavenly mindset and attitude. Some preachers declare that one day we will all dwell together in unity in Heaven. I would like to go further than that. We are meant to have such unity on earth now and are supposed to do all we can to maintain it and live in it. Jesus announced that all men everywhere would know, without a doubt, that we are His disciples *when we display His kind of love to one another.*

The Greek word for "love" used here by John the apostle is *agape*.

To reduce this down to a simple explanation it means "God's kind of love", a love that is not self-seeking and is unconditional. God loves you. It's His choice to love you. His love for you is not based upon what you do for Him, it is unconditional. There are no conditions! If you reject Him, He will still love you. If you sin, His love will find you and heal you. His love sent His Son Jesus to die in your place because He loved you before you were even born or made one mistake. Jesus came to rescue you before you knew you were lost, because His love reaches out even to those who will not respond or receive it. That may not be Hollywood's kind of love, but it is God's kind and it's meant to be our kind of love.

The Lord's Table is a place where unconditional love and forgiveness is expressed freely. If my brother has fallen out with me, or me with him, then I am meant to reach out in some way to bring reconciliation that we might enjoy the very best of that which is on God's table of provision. We have spent millions of sterling pounds, dollars, yen and every other currency to make tracts, books, films and music albums about His love and still the division increases in the Church and effective evangelism diminishes. Doing whatever it takes to heal the rifts between people and churches to help strengthen the body in our locality, region and the world would do more to express the message of God's love than all the sermons in the world.

A turning point

In 1977 I found myself standing in the middle of the night at the top of a 220ft cliff. It was the bleakest moment of my entire life and I could see no reason to carry on living. I couldn't find a reason to wake up one more morning and live one more day where my heart was broken, lost, empty of faith and hope, without the sense of being significant to anyone. I had been raised in the Church all of my life. I had sung the hymns, heard the sermons and taken communion. But nothing touched my heart. I saw no reason to live. I thought that if I was of no real value or significance to anyone then there was no purpose for living.

I stepped forward to jump off the cliff when suddenly I heard a voice behind me call out, "This is not My will for you. Go home and I will reveal it to you." Shocked, I stepped back and turned around. The voice spoke again, comforting me, but I saw no one. I thought I was alone in the darkness, but clearly I was not. The voice was somehow familiar and as it spoke peace returned to my heart. All anxiety and feelings of insignificance left me as the Lord revealed Himself to me. His love overwhelmed me. I couldn't believe the God of the Bible was right there with me in the bleakest moment of my life. The more He talked the more I became aware that He had a great plan for my life that was so good it was hard for me to comprehend. I went home, nervously wondering what my wife would be thinking. It was 1.00am and I expected her to be angry, wondering what I'd been up to until one in the morning. But I was going to be shocked by what awaited me when I walked through the door of my house that night as my world was being rocked.

Anne, my wife, was busy doing some chores, not in bed as I expected. She was so excited to see me that it disarmed and unsettled me for a moment. She began explaining that she had seen the first half of a film on television called *Jesus of Nazareth*. She spoke of how I would have enjoyed it. She spoke of the miracles and about the look in Jesus' eyes – that He just seemed to "know" what people were feeling and going through! Then, out of her mouth came the words that made me realize the Lord was doing something not just with me, but Anne also.

Anne had always maintained she was an atheist and that there was no God. She had never attended a church except to see her brother John singing solo or in a choir. Yet, here she was gushing about this film. Then she told me it had impacted her so much that she had got down on her knees and prayed for the first time. "God, if you exist, show me," she had said. "If it's true that Jesus was Your Son, then show me." On the same night at the very same moment both Anne and I were being touched and confronted by a God who loved us.

She could see by now the tears welling up in my eyes as she talked. I was too nervous to explain exactly what had happened to me in case she thought I was mad. I also thought she would be hurt to hear I had gone somewhere to commit suicide. So I didn't tell her that night. Instead I made some sort of excuse for my lateness and explained that the tears were because I was so happy for her.

Anne had made arrangements for us to visit my sister, Rhiannon, and her family the following Sunday. The plan was that we would watch the second half of the film together with the rest of the family. As we sat and watched it I understood why she had found it so compelling. I was gripped by Jesus' voice, the miracles and the horrendous scene of the crucifixion. I sat there trying to quash the emotions that began to erupt within me to prevent them from exploding in front of the family. I wanted to stand up and scream out loud, "You don't kill the good guy, you kill the bad one!" But my sense of pride or fear made me keep swallowing the emotions until I thought my head would explode. I "white knuckled" almost the entire film.

Throughout the film, as I watched a depiction of Jesus on the screen, the voice I'd heard on the cliff-top was talking to me. Now I knew for sure that I wasn't mad, I was hearing the voice of Jesus telling me that He died to forgive my sin and take away my shame. I knew at that very moment that He would gladly have done it all *just for me* if He needed to. I had always believed He had done it for "everyone", but it had never penetrated my heart or understanding that His sacrifice was more than just for "everyone else" – it was for me! He loved me. He loved me just as I was, right there and then. As the nails were hammered into His hands and feet so I felt what seemed like a searing hot knife or sword penetrate and twist within my heart. As it twisted I wanted to scream "Forgive me!" from the depths of my being. As the credits began to roll up at the end of the film, I grabbed my coat and told my wife and son, Matthew, to get in the car because we were heading home immediately. Everyone was surprised because we were all meant to enjoy a meal together. My family tried to persuade me to stay, but I knew that if I didn't go home then I had no idea what would happen to me.

Anne, Matthew and I arrived home, and as soon as I got through the front door I fell on the floor crying, "Jesus, forgive me … Jesus, forgive me!" I lay there for hours, crying the same thing over and over. I prayed what later I discovered was a "prayer of salvation". I had never heard one before so it just came from my heart. I prayed something like, "Jesus, I have made a miserable mess of my life and I can't fix it. Please come into my life and change it. Do whatever you need to do to fix it." Right at that moment someone walked through the walls of that tiny house in Wales and touched me. As He touched me every bit of guilt, shame, heaviness and emptiness left me. *And I knew it had!* Real peace flooded and filled my soul for the first time in my life.

When I got to my feet I was surprised to see Anne sitting there watching me, with tears running down her face. I had no idea that hours had passed by in what seemed like just a few minutes. She had watched me, feeling helpless to know what to say or do for me. I told her then of my experience on the cliff top the week before and how I had heard a voice that I now knew was the voice of Jesus. She too knew someone had walked into our home that night. She heard my voice change from someone pleading for help to someone surrendering their life to Jesus. It so touched her heart that from that moment she began to pray to the Lord and read her Bible. Just a few months later she gave her heart and life to the Lord and together we began a twenty-four year journey of incredible change that affected many hundreds of thousands of people before her death eventually parted us in 2001.

I share this story to show that all the sermons, songs and sacraments I had heard had not touched me. All it took was a moment in which the God of the universe stepped into my life with an act of love and compassion and gave me a sense of significance. His one act of love expressed more to me than all the sermons, songs and sacraments I had ever experienced.

This is what I plead today whenever I preach, that we become His body, His family, and that we act like one, not like we are strangers or estranged from one another, or involved in some childish competition to be the "No.1" church in town. Division will be healed when people begin to cross the divide with acts of agape love. Some people or churches will never receive your love the way it is intended and will wish to remain divided and that's a shame. But the Bible asks us in Romans 12:18, *"If it is possible, as much as depends on you, live peaceably with all men."* We cannot *make* someone else be reconciled with us, but we can do whatever we need to do to bring reconciliation. We can do our bit.

So, next time you are invited to take part in the Lord's Table, take a moment to remember the message behind the sacrament. Remember He loved you so much that He stepped out of Heaven, His home, to go through terrible pain so that your sin could be wiped out and forgotten by a Father who loves you. He didn't make you pay the price, He paid it for you. Is there someone in your life today that you need to be reconciled with? Don't wait for them to pay the price to put it right, you pay it for them and go to them and do all you can to be reconciled.

Are there churches in your town that are struggling? Does your church have an abundance of the very thing they need? Why not go to them as a church and give out of what you have to help them grow and fulfill their vision. If you are the leader of a church, what are you doing to remove the division or disunity from the body of Christ?

We are stronger together than we are apart. When the Word of God says we can accomplish more together than apart – *"one can chase a thousand, and two put ten thousand to flight"* (Deuteronomy 32:30) – which one of us is going to explain to the Lord that we preferred to do it alone instead of His way? Pick up your phone, write a letter or an email, send a gift or even visit the one who has offended you or fallen out with you. Get things put right as best you can, because unity and forgiveness is the key to moving from Bethany and Bethphage to your Jerusalem.

CHAPTER 16

IN ONE MOMENT EVERYTHING WILL TURN AROUND

In chapter 9 we briefly discussed the verses from Mark 16 where Jesus appears to two of His disciples on the Emmaus Road. I said then that I would return to these verses later, after we had examined the events of the four days preceding them. Now we understand more of what happened on the days immediately preceding Jesus' death and burial, let us look at the message these verses contain.

*"Now when He rose early on the first day of the week, He **appeared** first to Mary Magdalene, out of whom He had cast seven demons. She went and told those who had been with Him, as they mourned and wept. And when they heard that He was alive and had been seen by her, **they did not believe**. After that, **He appeared** in **another form** to two of them as they walked and went into the country. And they went and told it to the rest, **but they did not believe them either**. Later **He appeared** to the eleven as they sat at the table; and **He rebuked their unbelief and hardness of heart, because they did not believe** those who had seen Him after He had risen."* (Mark 16:9-14)

On the third day, on the Sunday morning, Jesus rose from the dead. Mary had returned to the tomb at daybreak to finish embalming His body. That is, after all, what you do to someone who is dead – you dress them for burial, then you bury them. You don't expect them to live again! Because of the lateness of the hour when Jesus was first placed in the tomb Mary had not been able to complete the embalming process. So she had arranged to come back after the Sabbath was over and the Feast of Passover was finished. Returning she found, to her amazement, the tomb open and the body of Jesus missing. She was rightly hysterical at that thought that anyone could do such a horrendous thing as to steal or move the body of her closest friend in the midst of her grief. Pain gripped her soul. As if watching Him die was not enough, she was now unexpectedly and inexplicably experiencing a new depth of anguish, as though she was watching Him die for a second time. Wasn't once enough for anyone?

No doubt she screamed and gripped the stone that had once covered the entrance to the tomb. But why was it hurting Mary in particular so much? Many theologians believe Mary had been a prostitute. If so, then men had paid so they could get something from her. More and more men had visited her, lustfully taking and using her body. She had not known what it was to feel genuine love from a man who wanted nothing from her. No man in her life had wanted only to give her respect, dignity, significance and security – until, that is, Jesus had come into her life those few years before. For the first time in her life she experienced a genuine, unconditional love lavished upon her. Now, the One who had given *real life* to her was gone. And not only was He dead, His body was missing. At least she had consoled herself with the thought that whenever she was vulnerable or confused she could return, lean upon the stone, touch the walls of His tomb and picture Him smiling reassuringly at her, as He always used to. He would be untouchable, but still near by. But now that had been taken away from her!

The Passover is more than a memorial service

As those around her laid the lamb upon the table, carving portions and placing them on people's plates, tearing the bread and passing it between them, Mary could think of nothing but the One who had changed her life. As finally the cup of wine was passed from one person to another, and the salutations that accompanied the ritual were spoken, she could think of nothing but being near the One who loved her so graciously. This ritual of the Feast of Passover meant nothing to her in comparison to the love she felt for her Lord and Master who had been so viciously crucified before her eyes.

She looked along the table and saw the unfolding of the Scriptures from as far back as Israel's captivity and bondage to Egypt. She saw how, on that very first night, Israel had been instructed by God, through Moses, to initiate the Feast of Passover. They were to take a pure, spotless lamb from amongst the flock, strip it of its wool, tie its feet and legs in order to stop it moving, scourge its back with many lines and cuts and finally roast it above a fire in full view of everyone in the house. Then they were to take a bowl of its blood and paint it upon the doorframe. All the people of Israel were to go into their houses and at midnight eat the meal in somber mood, dressed as if ready to move suddenly, whilst above and around them the Angel of Death came across the land and all the firstborn, man and beast, that were not inside the "protected" houses died. That night Egypt's might, power and control died never to rise again, while Israel rose again into a new life of freedom, set free from their bondage, leaving Egypt with the wealth of the people in their hands and heading for a journey that should have lasted just eleven days, but turned into forty years in the wilderness.

Mary, not meaning to be disrespectful, watched, grieving, feeling it was just a meaningless exercise of ritual, saying to herself, "But what does it all mean?" If only someone at that point could have whispered in her ear, as my friend Kevin did in mine all those years ago, "What do you think it is?" Would her eyes have been opened to a new perspective of seeing, enabling her to grasp the truth hidden behind the feast and the ritual? She had not connected the dots yet. She had not realized that the traditional Feast of

Passover pointed not just to Israel's past, but was a sign pointing to what God's Passover Lamb – *"the Lamb of God who takes away the sin of the world"* (John 1:29) – was about to do for all mankind. She was unable to see the parallels between the natural Feast of history and the spiritual Feast that Jesus fulfilled and became.

He had been taken from amongst His flock that fateful night in the garden on the Mount of Olives and had entered Jerusalem through the same gate, at the same time, that the natural Passover lamb was being taken through. As the natural Passover lamb was being prepared for his slaughter to pay for the price of Israel's sin, so God's Passover Lamb was being prepared to give His life. He would not just cover over the sin of the world, but pay for it, remove it and obliterate it, so that it need never again stand between a Father in Heaven and his wayward children.

As Levites and Priests inspected their lambs, so Pilate inspected Jesus, God's Lamb, only to find Him pure, declaring *"I find no fault in him"* (John 18:38). He had been stripped of his clothing, just as the lamb was stripped of its wool. He was tied to a post and whipped, just as the lamb was scourged, and left with thirty nine stripes plus one across His body. The whips the Romans used on Him had chunks of metal, glass and even nails woven into the strands of leather which lashed around His body literally tearing His flesh off His torso and face. When it was finished, Isaiah's prophesy had truly been fulfilled. He was beyond recognition (Isaiah 52:14). Both lambs were placed on wood in full view of everyone, one over a natural fire, one on a cross, hung up for all to see, experiencing the flames of a painful and humiliating death with grace, humility and dignity. But He blamed no one and forgave everyone, regardless of their sin, color, race, gender, generation or their acceptance or rejection of His love and sacrifice for them. He embraced it all willingly, knowing it was the only way for man to be saved from the fires of an eternal Hell.

Mary could not see that although Israel had celebrated the Feast each year since that first occasion in Egypt, they had never again experienced what happened that first night. Like the majority of others, she had not detected the message of death and resurrection that was hidden within the ritual. Mary could see the death, but not the victory, deliverance or resurrection that had been prophesied. So, three days later when viewing an empty tomb, she didn't expect to see Jesus alive.

She needed to understand and look at the empty tomb with a new perspective, but at the moment she just couldn't see what was happening in front of her. She turned to plead with someone nearby, who she thought was a gardener, asking if he knew what had happened to the body of Jesus. Standing before her was the very One she was looking for. She had walked past the living Jesus to visit a dead one. She had gone to where she had last left Him, but He had moved address. She was distraught, her heart longing to see Him one more time. Someone had robbed her of the one thing she had dreamed of for three days whilst trapped in family traditions and culture: holding Him just one more time to look on His face, touch His hands, wipe His hair away from His face and kiss Him farewell.

He is a God of no limitations

Mary didn't recognize Jesus when she first saw Him, though she had seen Him probably every day since He first stepped into her life. She cooked His meals, mended His clothes, sat at His feet listening to every single word He said. She probably, like every woman I know, watched His mannerisms, analyzed His face, knew the color of His eyes, and noticed any blemishes or distinguishing features. She would even have known His smell. Men don't understand any of this as it is a woman thing. We would remember the events, the highlights, the jokes, the storms, the steaks etc. But Mary would have known His every like, dislike, dream and desire. Yet, she didn't recognize Him now. How could His appearance have changed? All she wanted was to understand.

Jesus was asking her to see with a new perspective. He simply spoke her name: "Mary!" He knew her and as she heard His voice she also knew it was Him. All His compassion, tenderness and intimacy flowed through that one word. She heard the voice of her Lord and yet her eyes played tricks on her. Her heart and spirit knew it was Him, but she didn't recognize Him. Then, as she scrutinized His face, she looked into His eyes and they seemed to become like windows. Suddenly, in the blink of an eye she knew. She saw. It all made sense now. Grief turned to jubilation, despair to hope. What looked like the end had instead become a new beginning. The story of Passover was not history, but reality, and it didn't end with a death, but initiated a resurrection – and not just for Jesus, but for all who would believe and come to His house in their midnight moment of life. It was Jesus! It didn't look like Him, but it was Him, just in another form.

Mary flung herself at Jesus was about to wrap her arms around Him when He stepped out of her grasp. It wasn't that He didn't want her to hold Him, but He didn't want her to cling onto Him for the wrong reason. As she moved towards Him with tears running down her face, thoughts flashed through her mind: "You lost Him once, don't lose Him again." She was going to grab hold of Jesus tightly and never let Him go. But He was not prepared for her to keep Him in her "box" to appease her soul and meet her needs. He had done miracles to get people out of their "boxes", whether they were literal coffins and graves or diseases and demon-possession. He had just stepped out of His grave. He was not going to be put back into man's box of experience, knowledge or theology. He was going to make a demand upon His followers to accept that He could not be put in a box of limitations to suit them, but instead was going to require them to step out of their boxes of understanding into a life they never knew existed – God's kind of Life!

Then, just as suddenly as He'd appeared, He was gone. He vanished into thin air. Jesus after the cross was doing something He had never done before the cross! He changed His appearance and was able to disappear and appear elsewhere in a split second. But in one moment Jesus had turned Mary's life around from brokenness to wholeness, from grief to joy, from death to life. She ran as fast as she could to tell her friends the good news that Jesus was not dead, but alive. It was going to challenge everything the disciples had ever known. They were going to have to learn that God wants us to let go of everything we have ever known, to lay hold of everything we have ever dreamed of.

CHAPTER 17

LET GO OF EVERYTHING YOU HAVE EVER KNOWN, TO LAY HOLD OF EVERYTHING YOU HAVE EVER DREAMED OF

As two of Jesus' disciples walked away from Jerusalem, the Bible says they were busy debating with one another when Jesus appeared next to them. A debate is when two people of differing opinions on the same issue both argue their point of view. We don't know exactly what they were debating, but from the Bible narrative it is natural to conclude they were discussing the events of the past few days and were confused, with differing opinions about what it all meant. To one the cross was a defeat, to the other it was a victory. One argued that Jesus showed He was a King, whilst the other argued Jesus was to be the Suffering Servant. One believed Jesus would have an earthly kingdom, the other remained steadfast in believing His was an eternal kingdom.

The passionate, heated debate continued while Jesus appeared in their midst, right in the middle of them! Whenever we are passionate to understand the truth Jesus will appear and open our eyes. He promised us, *"Ask, and it will be given to you; seek, and you will find; knock, and it will be opened to you. For everyone who asks receives, and he who seeks finds, and to him who knocks it will be opened."* (Matthew 7:7-8)

With one disciple either side of Him, Jesus unfolded the Scriptures to show He was not on one side of the debate or the other, but both. He was both King and Servant. His Kingdom was on earth and in Heaven. The cross was both an end and a new beginning, a closing and an opening. Their hearts warmed within them, but they didn't recognize Him. Why not? Had they not followed Him for some three years? Had they not sat and learned from Him, seen the miracles? Had they not been in the upper room? But the narrative says He appeared to them in "another form" (Mark 16:12), so we can't blame them for not recognizing Him! He didn't look like the Jesus they had known so well. He had changed.

They only discovered that they were listening to Jesus later, when they had persuaded Him to stay for a meal in their house. Suddenly He picked up the bread, thanked the Lord for it, broke it and gave it to them, proceeding to do the same with the cup of wine. He was using the same language and actions He had used during the Last Supper. They must have looked at each other, wondering how this stranger could possibly know what Jesus had done in the upper room the night He was betrayed by Judas. They looked longingly into His face, their hearts broken with disappointment and grief as this man brought back the memories of that painful night, aching to have some sort of answer to all they had been through.

But as they looked, they saw something. Could it be possible? Could this really be Jesus? Faith was rising in their hearts. Faith was asking them to believe what they could not see with their eyes. In fact, what they saw with their eyes challenged everything they were experiencing within. They put their hope in faith and immediately their eyes opened. At last they knew it was Jesus, but once again He vanished from sight. Suddenly, instead of arguing and debating, they both began to encourage each other by reminding themselves of the things they had experienced as they walked with this man the seven miles from Jerusalem to Emmaus. Their hearts had been warmed as Jesus unpacked the Scriptures to reveal the life, death and even the resurrection of the Messiah

– the One who would be known as the Christ.

Then they ran, just as Mary had done when her eyes were opened. They ran with speed, each trying to be the first to spread the good news of His resurrection. So will we when our eyes are truly opened. It is such a compelling truth and reality that it demands us to go with speed. Isn't that another truth revealed in the Passover? They ate the Passover meal dressed ready to leave Egypt in a hurry with their clothes tucked into their belts and a staff in their hands. Mary and these two disciples had feasted on the *real* Passover Lamb on the first day of the week and they moved in haste to tell the others. As the Emmaus disciples arrived at the upper room they found it filed with shock, disbelief and confusion and discovered that Mary had arrived before them to tell the incredible news that Jesus was alive.

I am sure these two disciples could not understand why everyone was not rejoicing as they and Mary were. The reason was simple. They had *seen,* the others had not. It is easy to get impatient and frustrated with those who cannot see what is so obvious to us. But then, they only saw because Jesus came to where they were and helped them take a leap of faith of massive proportions. Then their eyes were opened!

Much was being challenged in that upper room. Logic said it was impossible for Jesus to be alive when they had buried Him. Had they forgotten Lazarus? Or the boy outside the village of Nain? Perhaps they reasoned that it was only Jesus, when He was alive, who had such faith to pray and see the dead raised. Now He was dead, who could have faith capable of raising Him up? Obviously none of them.

The Lord also challenged their culture, theology and experience by using a woman to be the very first witness to His resurrection. Some of their struggle to believe was surely to do with the person through whom the message came. Not because it was Mary, but simply because women were distinctly second class citizens in their society, despite the fact that Jesus had challenged this attitude constantly with His teaching and practice. From a legal standpoint, the testimony of a woman was not valid in a court of law. Would they therefore be willing to let go of their logic, the limitations of their experience and theology they had grown up with, and instead receive this truth that would forever transform their lives?

But now here came two more "witnesses" to Jesus' resurrection to confirm everything Mary had told them. Now what do they do? Peter and John had already run to the tomb to see if what Mary said was the truth. They had seen the empty tomb and the bandages lying neatly folded, but saw nothing else. They looked at the natural circumstances but didn't see beyond them. Accompanying them, Mary stepped into the same tomb moments later and saw two angels, one at each end of the bed where Jesus had lain. The picture was not wasted on her. She knew from drawings and teachings of old of the Ark of the Covenant that had been made during the time of Moses which had led Israel from Egypt all the way through the wilderness to Canaan. The top of that Ark was made of pure gold. It was like a slab or a table and was called the Mercy Seat. At each end there was an angel. The face of each angel looked down upon the blood of the Passover lamb that was poured out upon the Mercy Seat by the High Priest. Here, in Jesus' tomb, was a bloodstained slab with an angel at each end.

It's amazing that both sets of people had entered the same tomb. Peter and John had only surveyed the scene with natural eyes, but Mary's eyes were opened to see beyond the natural. She was now learning to live in the arena of two worlds – the temporal and the eternal, the seen and the unseen. She was discovering that the unseen, eternal world had no limitations as Jesus began to break all the laws of natural life, physics, science and gravity. But she knew that this was just the beginning. There was more she was yet to learn and her heart ached within her as she contemplated all that could possibly lie ahead of her.

Is this how you feel?

We have a choice to make. We can continue to live our Christian life rooted in the seen world, relying on our natural abilities and philosophies and affect just a few people in our world. Or, like Mary, we can make ourselves ready and willing to embrace the rollercoaster life of God. One existence will keep us safe and saved, but stuck. The other can transport us out of our life of limitation into the incredible arena of His unlimited, uncontainable life and power.

Remember, *don't kick your donkey, ride it!* Remember that God is using the circumstances of your life to help you transition into the fullness of your destiny in Him. Learn to allow the challenges of life to equip you with what you need to step across the thresholds of fear and limitation into all that God has prepared ahead of you!

Further information

There is a sequel to Don't Kick the Donkey, Ride it! Look out for the next book in this series: Alignment for Assignment. This book looks at how Jesus changed His appearance many times, purposefully, to reveal more of Himself to us and to bring us into alignment with the eternal life of God and His kingdom.

Join

Wynne & Gwenda

Out & About!

inHOPE Leadership Schools

inHOPE Conferences

Ministering in Churches

Radio & TV Programs

DVD/CD Teaching Packs

For Full Itinerary & resources go to
www.wynnegoss.com
email: admin@wynnegoss.com or
look us up on Facebook

Published by *in*HOPE Publishing